Employing People with Disabilities

Ewa Giermanowska · Mariola Racław ·
Dorota Szawarska

Employing People with Disabilities

Good Organisational Practices and Socio-cultural Conditions

Ewa Giermanowska
Institute of Applied Social Sciences
University of Warsaw
Warsaw, Poland

Mariola Racław
Institute of Applied Social Sciences
University of Warsaw
Warsaw, Poland

Dorota Szawarska
Institute of Applied Social Sciences
University of Warsaw
Warsaw, Poland

ISBN 978-3-030-24551-1   ISBN 978-3-030-24552-8 (eBook)
https://doi.org/10.1007/978-3-030-24552-8

© The Editor(s) (if applicable) and The Author(s), under exclusive license to Springer Nature Switzerland AG 2020
This work is subject to copyright. All rights are solely and exclusively licensed by the Publisher, whether the whole or part of the material is concerned, specifically the rights of translation, reprinting, reuse of illustrations, recitation, broadcasting, reproduction on microfilms or in any other physical way, and transmission or information storage and retrieval, electronic adaptation, computer software, or by similar or dissimilar methodology now known or hereafter developed.
The use of general descriptive names, registered names, trademarks, service marks, etc. in this publication does not imply, even in the absence of a specific statement, that such names are exempt from the relevant protective laws and regulations and therefore free for general use.
The publisher, the authors and the editors are safe to assume that the advice and information in this book are believed to be true and accurate at the date of publication. Neither the publisher nor the authors or the editors give a warranty, expressed or implied, with respect to the material contained herein or for any errors or omissions that may have been made. The publisher remains neutral with regard to jurisdictional claims in published maps and institutional affiliations.

Cover illustration: © Melisa Hasan

This Palgrave Pivot imprint is published by the registered company Springer Nature Switzerland AG
The registered company address is: Gewerbestrasse 11, 6330 Cham, Switzerland

Acknowledgements

The authors wish to thank the people thanks to whom this book was written, and who accompanied us in the implementation of the research project and further work involved in the analysis of the results. We would like to thank Professor Barbara Gąciarz from the Faculty of Humanities of the AGH University of Science and Technology in Krakow, whose substantive and organisational involvement enabled us to conceptualize the project and carry out empirical research. We owe our thanks to Joanna Kotzian and Magdalena Pancewicz, consultants from the HRK S.A. company, whose experience in consulting work and the ability to interact with employers allowed us to acquire unique empirical material. Colleagues from the Institute of Applied Social Sciences of the University of Warsaw, the Faculty of Humanities at AGH and the Institute of Sociology of the Jagiellonian University offered in-depth discussion about the project results, especially in relation to their public perception.

CONTENTS

1 Introduction 1
   1 Background to the Book 1
   2 Disability 2
   3 Employment 3
   4 Good Practices at Work 4
   5 The Structure of the Book 5
   References 8

2 Work and Employment of People with Disabilities:
Towards a Social Model 9
   *1 The Change of the Paradigm in the Approach
to the Phenomenon of Disability* 9
   *2 Employment of Disabled People in the Light of Statistics
and Employment Support Models* 16
   *3 Determinants of the Employment Policy of Disabled People
as a Public Policy* 28
   References 34

3 Multivariate Conditions of Introducing People
with Disabilities to the Labour Market: Coupled
Impact and the Effect of Synergy 37
   *1 The History of Sanctioning Non-employment of People
with Disabilities* 37

    1.1   *The Real Nature of Disability and Its Determinants*   37
    1.2   *Exclusion from the Labour Market and New*
         Perspectives   44
  2 *The Results of the Research Identifying Factors of Activity*
     of People with Disabilities on the Labour Market   48
  3 *"Bundle of Factors" Model*   58
  References   61

4 Good Practices as a Tool for Modelling Employer Policies from the Open Labour Market   67
  1 *The Importance of Human Resources Management in Relation to People with Disabilities*   67
    1.1   *Functions of Human Resources Policy*   67
    1.2   *International Documents on Disability Management in the Workplace*   70
    1.3   *Diversity Management and CSR*   74
  2 *Good Practices in Research on Employing People with Disabilities*   83
    2.1   *Definition of Good Practices*   83
    2.2   *Examples of Research Reports on Good Practices*   87
  References   93

5 Good Practices in the Personnel Management Process   97
  1 *Research Methodology*   97
  2 *Recruitment and Induction*   101
  3 *Adapting the Workplace and Assistantship*   111
  4 *Keeping the Employee in Employment and Employee Development*   115
  5 *Disability Management in the Workplace*   121
  6 *Employer's Image and Disability*   126
  7 *Good Practices Raising Doubts: The Negative Side of Good Practices*   130
  References   134

6 **Conclusions and Recommendations** 139
   *1 The Importance of Diffusion of Good Practices
     and the Sociocultural Context* 141
   *2 Scientific Knowledge and Its Importance in Changing
     the Social World* 147
   References 152

Index 155

LIST OF FIGURES

Chapter 2

Fig. 1 Employment rate of people by type of disability in % (20–64), 2011 (*Source* European Commission: http://appsso.eurostat.ec.europa.eu/nui/show.do?dataset=hlth_dlm010&lang=en [accessed 14 January 2019])   19

Fig. 2 Employment rate of people by type of disability in % (20–64), 2011 males (*Source* European Commission: http://appsso.eurostat.ec.europa.eu/nui/show.do?dataset=hlth_dlm010&lang=en [accessed 14 January 2019])   19

Fig. 3 Employment rate of people by type of disability in % (20–64), 2011 females (*Source* European Commission: http://appsso.eurostat.ec.europa.eu/nui/show.do?dataset=hlth_dlm010&lang=en [accessed 14 January 2019])   20

Chapter 3

Fig. 1 The phenomenon of disability in the conceptualization of ICIDH (*Source* Based on World Health Organization 1980)   42

Fig. 2 Interactions between the components of the ICF (*Source* Based on World Health Organization 2001)   43

Fig. 3 "Bundle of factors" model (*Source* Own analysis)   58

Chapter 6

Fig. 1 Factors influencing good practices among employers
(*Source* Own analysis) 146

Fig. 2 Multivariate nature of good organisational practices.
*(a) preparing people with disabilities for entering the labour market and retaining employment and (b) preparing employers to employ people with disabilities (*Source* Own analysis) 147

List of Tables

Chapter 2

Table 1 Employment rate by type of disability by age in % (2011) 21

Chapter 3

Table 1 Selected factors from various levels of social organisation affecting the activity of people with disabilities 59

Chapter 6

Table 1 Examples of good practices in various areas of HRM 142

CHAPTER 1

Introduction

Abstract This chapter serves as an introduction to the topic of the book, namely good practices and sociocultural context in the employment of people with disabilities in a rapidly changing world. We consider the main areas organizing the structure of the book: disability, employment and good practices at work. We also provide an overview of the different chapters.

Keywords Disability · Employment · Good practices

1 BACKGROUND TO THE BOOK

In this book, we consider the questions of what are good practices and what functions do they have in different sociocultural contexts? We point to the fact that good employment practices in the area of disability are directly linked with the issue of vocational activation of people with disability. These issues have to be analysed together in order to develop or assess existing good practices. For example, if good practices in the area of recruitment are to be effective, people with disabilities need to be motivated enough and consider themselves capable enough, to participate in the recruitment process.

We point to the various aspects of sociocultural context that have an impact on the shape and effectiveness of good practices and develop a multivariate, multidimensional model of factors influencing the

© The Author(s) 2020
E. Giermanowska et al., *Employing People with Disabilities*,
https://doi.org/10.1007/978-3-030-24552-8_1

professional activation and employment of workers with disabilities. The model may also be applied when developing or analysing good practices.

This book grew out of and was inspired by a research project carried out in the years of 2012–2014 dealing with the employment of disabled workers in Poland and across Europe in relation to good practices applied by employers. In the original project, the data analysis published in 2014 (Giermanowska 2014) deals with, above all, the level of the organisations. Here, we consider the problem of good practices in relation to disability, in a wider social and cultural context, including, but not limited to, the organisational one.

The book is largely organized around the following areas, the overview of which is presented below: disability, employment and good practices.

2 Disability

How disability is defined in society and the state has a direct impact on the position and role of the disabled, and any obligations that might exist towards them. As is apparent from the analysis presented in Chapter 2 of this book, what we are currently observing is a dynamic shift in the perception of disability and the disabled as a social group, especially in terms of employment. The language used in relation to disabled workers by employers, HR managers but also policy makers are changing from that of minority protection to diversity management of the workforce. In a similar fashion, the accent is changing from oppression, exclusion and dependency, towards the agency of people with disabilities, self-determination, dignity and independence. This does not mean of course that exclusion or dependency has been eradicated, as evidenced by, e.g., employment statistics, but that people with disabilities play an openly active role in shaping and changing their situation for the better and that their rights as citizens and workers are to be protected, promoted and respected by law and by employers.

This shift in the discourse somewhat obscures the fact that workers with disabilities form a very diverse group, that despite many improvements made recently, remains to some degree vulnerable. This applies particularly to people with intellectual disabilities, but not exclusively. Therefore, some amount of care needs to be extended in order to ensure their rights and protect from discrimination and abuse. That is somewhat problematic, as there exists a certain asymmetry between equality, which we strive for, for all of the workers, and care (see Tronto 2013), which results in mixed messages regarding the employment and treatment of workers with disability. On the one hand, we speak of equal opportunities, on the other, we formulate certain solutions created particularly in order to promote and protect disabled people at work, e.g. the quota system or good practices dedicated to workers with disabilities. One of the ways of dealing with this dissonance is to place all measures associated with the promotion and protections of disabled workers within the wider framework of diversity management, which by definition applies to all the workers. Good diversity management in part depends in convincing managers and employees that special measures applied in case of certain categories of workers benefit not only these workers, but everybody within the organisation and the society at large. However, this might not be easy, as the perception of people with disabilities and their position in society in general, and work environment in particular depends on multiple factors, as we explore in Chapter 3.

3 Employment

Work is one of the contexts in which people with disabilities may exercise their agency and gain economic independence, and especially in case of work on the open labour market, may participate in the wider social setting, which in the long run, might lead to normalization of disability. This makes employment of workers with disability priceless, as it benefits them and society on many different levels. Just as there are multiple factors influencing vocational activation and employment of people with disabilities, there are multidimensional and multi-level consequences of their employment (e.g. economic, social, psychological, health-related). This is of particular importance given the growing number of people with disabilities present in society.

The multivariate conditions affecting the employment of disabled workers discussed in Chapter 3 find their loci in workplaces. It is here that we see a meeting point of the major factors that matter: prejudice among co-workers and managers, ignorance of employers related to disabilities, legal obligations, possible sources of support or existing practical solutions, inflexibility of labour law, lack of flexibility and cooperation between various institutions meant to support people with disabilities, including health and rehabilitation facilities, limited qualifications of some disabled workers due to, e.g., limited access to education and training, sociocultural norms related to expectations as to what the disabled can and cannot achieve, and the quality of their work. But it is also workplaces and related organisations (including trade unions) that are the potential sites of developing practical solutions to the many obstacles present in employment of people with disabilities. It is at this level that both employers and employees must deal with uncertainty related to the employment of disabled workers, arising mostly out of ignorance and excessive focus on what people with disabilities cannot manage, rather than what they are capable of.

As the approach to disability changes within the society, so do the opportunities open to people with disabilities. In the past, access to education and training was limited due to various factors, now there is a growing number of better or even highly qualified people with disabilities. While the awareness of employers and readiness to employ workers with disabilities still lags behind the supply of qualified disabled workers, there is a growing recognition of disability as advantageous at work (Giermanowska et al. 2015). At the same time, the world of work and technological possibilities are rapidly evolving. On the one hand, what we mean by work is subject to change. On the other, new technological innovations mean that the impact of certain types of disability on the ability to work is decreasing. Both these factors that we touch upon in Chapter 3 have a positive impact on the position of disabled people at work and may be taken advantage of when designing company policy related to diversity management. This is of growing importance, particularly in Europe, given its decreasing and ageing population, and the growing number of highly qualified, educated and motivated people with disabilities.

4   Good Practices at Work

It is at this moment that we need to make absolutely clear that employment alone of workers with disabilities does not need to constitute good practice. Just as able-bodied workers, people with disabilities are in need of a meaningful employment according to their skills, capabilities and potential, leading to a dignified life, which at the same time needs to coincide with the interests of the employer.

This means, as we explore in Chapter 4, that on the one hand organisations need comprehensive adjustments of their practices on every level of human resource management (recruitment, induction, training and development, team building, reasonable adjustments, etc.), to meet the first condition mentioned above. At the same, good practices need to be considered in the wider organisational context, including the benefit to the organisation itself and the motivations for developing good practices. These might be linked with such things as corporate social responsibility and company branding, but equally they might be related to legislation requiring the equal treatment of workers on the labour market, and dwindling labour supply in certain areas.

As is apparent from the analysis of multivariate conditions in Chapter 3 and good practices presented in Chapters 4 and 5, if the solutions are to be effective and of benefit to everybody concerned, in their creation, assessment and implementation people from different levels of the company, including workers with disabilities, need to be engaged, as well as experts from outside organisations, specializing in supporting the employment of workers with disabilities given the local sociolegal and cultural context. This means that effective good solutions are usually tailor-made for particular organisations existing in particular contexts, which makes their direct transfer to other companies difficult. At the same time, it must be noted, their existence alone, especially in international corporations, leads to greater awareness of the fact they are needed, and therefore a more open attitude to their development and implementation, in various sites where such corporations operate. Moreover, because of the movement of workers, especially from the level of management, between companies, sectors and countries, the know-how related to the creation of good practices is spreading.

5 The Structure of the Book

The book, although written by academics, is directed towards a wider audience than merely an academic one. We wrote this book bearing in mind that a growing number of people, such as employers, managers of HR departments, organisations representing disabled persons, trade unions or representatives of self-government authorities, are actively engaged in planning, designing and implementing solutions related to the employment of people with disabilities and need to do it well. Some of them are experts in general HR management, while some are highly knowledgeable about the issues of rights and needs of disabled people, but we believe relatively few have a comprehensive knowledge of both disability issues and good business and HR practice. Which is why we include both a chapter on the concept of disability per se and in relation to employment and a chapter dealing with good business practice in relation to employment of people with disabilities. To this, we add a chapter (Chapter 3) that we believe to be a very useful roadmap in appreciating and understanding the wider social and cultural context and conditions affecting the employment of workers with disabilities. The detailed book structure is as follows.

The aim of Chapter 2, *Work and Employment of People with Disabilities: Towards a Social Model*, is to present the situation of people with disabilities on the labour market and conditions of contemporary public policy, with particular emphasis on the social and cultural context. Among others, the following issues will be discussed:

(a) The change of the paradigm defining disability and its institutionalization in international and community documents (WHO, UN, ILO, EU); evolution of views on ideas, with particular emphasis on the process of transition from the medical model to the social and sociomedical model; the role of international organisations; and employment and income of people with disabilities in international documents.
(b) The labour market of disabled people in the light of statistics; models of employment of people with disabilities in Europe (systems: quota, based on civic rights, motivating the employers); employer-oriented and disabled-person-oriented employment support instruments; and forms of employment of disabled people in an open and protected labour market.
(c) Determinants of public policy towards employment of people with disabilities; international and national legislation; sociocultural, economic and institutional conditions of employment of people with disabilities; and the specificity of employing people with disabilities in the countries of real communism and during the transformation of the system.

The aim of Chapter 3, *Multivariate Conditions of Introducing People with Disabilities on to the Labour Market: Coupled Impact and the Effect of Synergy*, is to analyse the bundles of factors affecting the employment of people with disabilities by companies and public institutions on domestic and local labour markets. We identify these factors in the subsystems of law, economy, society and culture, and organisational level of enterprises or labour market institutions (public/non-public). The impact of individual bundles of factors, e.g. the economic, sociocultural subsystems or organisational level, is already confirmed in theoretical and empirical studies.

At the same time, we refer to studies dealing with the evolution of employment forms of disabled people in feudal society and in industrial and post-industrial capitalism. We will also refer to the culturally sanctioned justifications of non-participation in the labour market of people with disabilities, causing social exclusion of people with disabilities. In the second half of the twentieth century, the practices of employing people with disabilities change. The practice of the "normalization" policy which aims to help people with disabilities achieve decent living conditions and valuable social roles is important. However, we point to its limitations.

The objective of our study will be to create a model showing the mutual and coupled impact of bundles of factors from individual groups and to demonstrate that the effect of employment for people with disabilities is a result of synergy. Difficulties in one sphere, such as economics, cannot be compensated directly by actions in another, such as the law. The principle of "connected vessels" does not work here. It is necessary to take into account the impact of all factors and strive to create the so-called strengthening effect (see Boudon 1979), accepting the supposition of intermediary variables in the creation of the employment effect.

In Chapter 4, *Good Practices as a Tool for Modelling Employer Policies from the Open Labour Market*, we define the concept of good practice in the field of employment of disabled people and the importance of diffusion of good practices for public policy and the policy of organisations (employers) from the public and private sectors. We also consider the importance of strategic personnel management (diversity management, CSR, etc.) and international documents on disability management in the workplace. Finally, we briefly present and discuss examples of research on good organisational practices in employing people with disabilities.

In Chapter 5, *Good Practices in the Personnel Management Process*, we carry out a secondary analysis of research results obtained as part of a project dealing with public policy of the state towards disability, implemented in 2012–2014. Research on good practices in employing disabled persons included employers (organisations) from the open labour market, from the private and public sectors. The chapter deals with, among others, issues such as:

- recruitment and induction,
- adapting the workplace and assistantship,
- keeping the employee in employment and employee development,
- disability management in the workplace,
- employer's image and disability,
- good practices raising doubts and the negative side of good practices.

In the final chapter, Chapter 6—*Conclusions and Recommendations*, we write about the importance of the engagement of employers and workers in the creation of good jobs for a diverse population in the dynamically changing world of work and the creation and spread of good practices. We also consider the role and possible contribution of social scientists in the analysis, creation and implementation of good practices and appropriate policy, especially in relation to the larger political and social context.

Public policy in the field of employing disabled people in Poland and Europe in recent years is changing and becoming more open to people with functional limitations. We are convinced that sociological research showing not only the economic but sociocultural context of employment of disabled people increases the sensitivity of public authorities, employers and the whole society, while at the same time demonstrating the complexity of the whole process. Disseminating good organisational practices among employers from different cultural and political circles is perhaps a small but important step in solving difficult social problems.

References

Boudon, Raymond. 1979. "Generating Models as a Research Strategy." In *Qualitative and Quantitative Social Research*, edited by Robert King Merton, James Samuel Coleman, and Peter Henry Rossi, 51–64. New York: The Free Press.

Giermanowska, Ewa, ed. 2014. *Zatrudniając niepełnosprawnych. Dobre praktyki pracodawców w Polsce i innych krajach Europy*. Kraków: Akademia Górniczo-Hutnicza im. S. Staszica w Krakowie.

Giermanowska, Ewa, Agnieszka Kumaniecka-Wiśniewska, Mariola Racław, and Elżbieta Zakrzewska-Manterys. 2015. *Niedokończona emancypacja – wejście niepełnosprawnych absolwentów szkół wyższych na rynek pracy*. Warszawa: Wydawnictwa Uniwersytetu Warszawskiego.

Tronto, Joan. 2013. *Caring Democracy: Markets, Equality and Justice*. New York: New York University Press.

CHAPTER 2

Work and Employment of People with Disabilities: Towards a Social Model

Abstract The aim of the chapter is to present the situation of people with disabilities on the labour market and conditions of contemporary public policy, with particular emphasis on the social and cultural context. Among others, the following issues will be discussed: the change of the paradigm defining disability and its institutionalization in international and community documents, the labour market of disabled people in the light of statistics and models of employment in Europe, determinants of public policy towards employment of people with disabilities.

Keywords Social model of disability ·
Statistics of employment of disability people ·
International and community documents ·
European models of employment of disability people ·
Determinants of the employment policy of disabled people

1 The Change of the Paradigm in the Approach to the Phenomenon of Disability

Researchers working on the phenomenon of disability emphasize changes in the way it is defined and perceived visible in most economically developed countries. There is a marked departure from perceiving disability as an individual moral flaw or health deficit in favour of perceiving its origin in the organisation of social life (Goodley 2011).

© The Author(s) 2020
E. Giermanowska et al., *Employing People with Disabilities*,
https://doi.org/10.1007/978-3-030-24552-8_2

This assumption lies at the heart of the social model. Responsibility for excluding people with disabilities from the main social institutions has been transferred from individuals to society. Disability is a socially constructed phenomenon. This means that it is influenced by historical, cultural and political factors that may exclude people with disabilities to a much greater degree than their physical and mental dysfunctions would (Oliver 1990, p. 22). According to this approach, disability results from the organisation of society, which limit the extent to which people with disabilities perform various social roles. As a consequence, people with disabilities remain excluded from the labour market and a number of public activities and are kept outside, whether hidden in special forms of education or permanent care institutions (Oliver 2009), the mainstream of social life. "By redefining disability as something created in the social world and not through biology (or genes or neurochemistry), the social model of disability enabled scholars (and activists and artists) to move disabled people away from their historical place in society as individuals in need of medical, rehabilitation, welfare, and other services and interventions to that of an oppressed social minority in need of recognition of its civil and human rights" (Rembis and Pamuła 2016).

In the literature on the subject, criticism of the social model is also becoming more common (Rembis and Pamuła 2016). Researchers pursuing the so-called Disability Studies (these are interdisciplinary, inter-sectional studies, focused on the activism of disabled people and social change) appear to be the main source of these critical arguments. According to them, the social model defines impairment as a biological reality that exists outside of social relations, politics and the pathologizing discourses of Western medicine (Rembis 2010/2015; Rembis and Pamuła 2016). Meanwhile, "Disability Studies theorists through their research and writing seek to promote change in all three areas related to disability – the built environment, social relations, and cultural perceptions" (Rembis and Pamuła 2016, p. 10).

Therefore, attempts are made to create a new paradigm that will respond to the limitations of both the medical model and the social model in analysing the phenomenon of disability and the process of locating people with functional deficits in the social structure. The medical model underestimated the impact of the fact and consequences of the social construction of disability, the social model is not sensitive enough to the diversity of experiences of people with disabilities, including the matter of pain or limitations related to the body. A biopsychosocial model was created that refers to the holistic concepts of understanding and explaining disability (Mikołajczyk-Lerman 2013, pp. 27–32). It emphasizes that disability is a multidimensional phenomenon that results from mutual interactions between people and their physical and social surroundings. It is the result of interaction between health determinants and the environment and particular characteristics of the individual. The biopsychosocial model assumes mutual and coupled influences of factors belonging to various areas and the principle of their modification due to the characteristics of the person subjected to these influences. Because disability is presented as a universal human experience, the risk of marginalization and labelling of persons with functional deficits is minimized.

At the level of social practice, the changes taking place in the sociocultural and political spheres (related to the definition and perception of the phenomenon of disability) are the result of actions of activists connected with the movement of disabled people, accompanied by the development of theoretical considerations. With regard to political actions, Barbara Gąciarz (2017, pp. 66–82) describes the cycle leading to the emergence of a new paradigm of public policies towards disability:

1. from activities inspired by the individual model, maintaining the control of rehabilitation and care institutions over persons with functional deficits (keeping them away from the economy and society),
2. through the emergence of the concept of normalization, based on the assumption of adapting people with disabilities to normal functioning in social life and having the largest range of social roles (see Sullivan 2011),
3. up to the emergence (on the initiative of bottom-up movements of people with disabilities) of the social model of disability as an international standard in terms of understanding the objectives of this policy and the most important ways of achieving them.

International regulations ensuring observance of the freedoms and human and civil rights of people with disabilities, including the right to work, are included in the documents of global organisations (United Nations, International Labour Organization) as well as European organisations (Council of Europe, European Union). The international community since the 1950s has come a long way in changing the perception of disability. It was connected with the increasing awareness of the international community of the problems of people with disabilities and a change in the approach, from one based on isolation and care, to one aimed at providing people with disabilities with the same opportunities as other members of society (Kurowski 2014, p. 40). The culmination of this process was the adoption by the United Nations General Assembly of the Convention on the Rights of Persons with Disabilities (CRPD). The Convention and its Optional Protocol were adopted on 13 December 2006 and entered into force on 3 May 2008.

The adoption of the Convention was the result of many years of work of international communities aimed at changing attitudes and approaches to persons with disabilities and who, on the international arena, struggled for a legal act regarding their rights.

"An International Disability Caucus has been created, which is a coalition of 70 international, regional and national organizations. UN member states and representatives of the disabled community cooperated on the UN forum in creating an appropriate treaty" (Kurowski 2014, p. 104[1]). The new dimension in the treatment of persons with disabilities, which the Convention sanctions, is the departure from the perception of people with disabilities as "objects" of mercy, treatment and social protection, to the perception of disabled people as "subjects" possessing rights, which they are able to claim, make decisions and be active members of society. This legal act is based on values arising from fundamental human rights. It guarantees people with disabilities equal access to institutions and the possibility of pursuing social activities and fulfilling the roles on the same principles as those who are able-bodied (Cotter 2007, p. 51).

Article 3 sets out the following principles on which the Convention is based:

a. Respect for inherent dignity, individual autonomy including the freedom to make one's own choices, and independence of persons;
b. Non-discrimination;
c. Full and effective participation and inclusion in society;
d. Respect for difference and acceptance of persons with disabilities as part of human diversity and humanity;
e. Equality of opportunity;
f. Accessibility;
g. Equality between men and women;

---

[1] Translation of the quote by D. Szawarska.

h. Respect for the evolving capacities of children with disabilities and respect for the right of children with disabilities to preserve their identities.

The recognition of the right of the disabled to work, including the right to maintain work freely chosen or accepted in a labour market and work environment that is open, inclusive and accessible to persons with disabilities is included in the Convention in the art. 27 Work and Employment. The Convention grants people with disabilities the right to work, on an equal basis with other people, and it is the state's duty to create an appropriate framework in order to create conditions conducive for the development of the labour market. In the case of the right to work of people with disabilities, it is particularly important to ensure equal treatment and access to work. Discrimination on the labour market of people with disabilities is particularly evident. In most countries, the unemployment rate of people with disabilities is higher than among the able-bodied, and the employment rate is definitely lower. People with disabilities are usually employed in low-paid jobs or on the protected labour market, and they have significantly limited freedom to choose a job and exercise their right to do so. Therefore, it became necessary to provide them with equal employment opportunities and to remove barriers limiting the right to work of people with disabilities. Article 27 of the Convention lists a series of actions (including legislative ones) which should be undertaken for this purpose: prohibiting discrimination in employment and guaranteeing protection of workers' rights to persons with disabilities on an equal basis with other citizens, enabling disabled people to use job counselling services and supporting their professional development (access to the labour market, career advancement), promoting employment in the public and private sectors and self-employment, ensuring rational adjustments at the workplace, promoting the acquisition of work experience, and providing services facilitating the return to work and maintaining employment.

The implementation of the right to work of people with disabilities, in accordance with the spirit of the Convention, thus consists in creating an institutional framework of the labour market, counteracting discrimination and equalizing opportunities by creating, in necessary situations, separate regulations for this group. Governments should undertake active measures for the professional integration of people with disabilities. These measures may also be applied to employers by creating incentives for employing workers with disabilities, as well as the general public to raise awareness and change attitudes towards people with disabilities.

In 2010, the European Commission adopted a communication establishing a Disability Strategy: "European Disability Strategy 2010–2020: A Renewed Commitment to a Barrier-Free Europe" (EDS). Its aim is to increase the opportunities of disabled people so that they can fully enjoy their rights and participate in social and economic life, on an equal basis. The strategy was created based on the *Convention on the Rights of Persons with Disabilities* (CRPD). In the introduction to the *Strategy* we read: "One in six people in the European Union (EU) has a disability that ranges from mild to severe making around 80 million who are often prevented from taking part fully in society and the economy because of environmental and attitudinal barriers. For people with disabilities the rate of poverty is 70% higher than the average partly due to limited access to employment" (EDS 2010–2020, p. 3).

The Strategy focuses on eliminating barriers. Eight areas of joint action between the EU and EU countries have been named:

- **Accessibility**: ensuring that people with disabilities have access to goods, services including public services and assistive devices;
- **Participation**: providing people with disabilities with full enjoyment of their basic rights, including the rights of the EU citizens;
- **Equality**: providing people with disabilities with protection against discrimination, and implementing an active policy of combating discrimination and promoting equal opportunities policy (both at EU and national levels);
- **Employment**: ensuring that a much greater number of people with disabilities has an opportunity to earn a living on the labour market and better access to employment;
- **Education and training**: development and spread of an education system open to all, and lifelong learning programmes for disabled pupils and students;
- **Social protection**: providing people with disabilities with access to social protection systems and other programmes, services and benefits preventing income inequality, poverty risk and social exclusion;
- **Health**: increasing equal access for disabled people to health services and related high-quality services;
- **External action**: promoting the rights of people with disabilities at an international level.

In the section of the Strategy devoted to employment, it was emphasized that only good work guarantees economic independence, stimulates personal achievement and provides the best protection against poverty. Therefore, many more people with disabilities must have access to the free labour market and earning an income from work. The European Commission has listed a number of measures to support national policies for better integration of disabled people. These include analysing the situation of disabled people in the labour market; fight against attitudes and traps associated with the use of services that discourage people with disabilities from entering the labour market; assistance in integration into the labour market through the use of the European Social Fund (ESF); developing an active labour market policy (ALMP); increasing the availability of jobs; developing services in the field of employment, supporting structures and training at the workplace. These measures should contribute to greater professional activity of disabled people, above all on the open labour market: "Enable many more people with disabilities to earn their living on the open labour market" (EDS 2010–2020, p. 7).

It should be emphasized that before the adoption of the "European Disability Strategy 2010–2020: A Renewed Commitment to a Barrier-Free Europe", provisions and documents promoting the participation of people with disabilities in various spheres of social life, including the open labour market, existed in relation to the member states (see Mokrzycka 2012). The discussed Strategy from 2010 is a continuation of Disability Action Plan (DAP EU) from 2003. This EU document in turn designated the scope of activities for disabled people in the years 2004–2010 in three phases. In the area of employment in phase I (2004–2005), the focus was on creating the conditions necessary to support employment of disabled people, in phase II (2006–2007) was on active inclusion and independence and in phase III was to introduce broadly understood access to labour market institutions. During the implementation of the DAP by member states, the Council of Europe developed the Action Plan CE (AP CE) for the years 2006–2015. It is an international document with a European range belonging to the so-called soft regulations. Section 3.5.1 deals with the issue of employing people with disabilities. Policy aiming to increase the professional activity rate of disabled people should take into account the diverse capabilities of these people, and it should be comprehensive, that is, aimed at abolishing existing barriers to access to the labour market. Employment issues for people with disabilities should be included in the general labour market policy of a given country on the principle of ensuring civic equality. In addition, an objective and individual assessment of the employment opportunities of people with disabilities should deal with their potential and not the degree of their disability. Hence. access to career counselling, job placement and activities related to returning to work for people with disabilities is necessary.

At the end of the twentieth century, there were also special European Community programmes. For example, "The Action Programme to assist disabled people", known as the "HELIOS II programme", was established by Council Decision 93/136/EEC of 25 February 1993. It covered the period from 1 January 1993 to 31 December 1996. It was a continuation of the "HELIOS I" programme (1988–1991). The HELIOS II programme addressed employment issues for people with disabilities. It was pointed out that new technologies allow better adaptation of workplaces to the needs of disabled people and facilitate their mobility (Dunay et al. 2016, p. 427). During this period, the role of the EU was not directional and was incidental, based on recommendation (Hvinden and Halverson 2003). Since the mid-1990s, the EU creates a broader disability policy strategy and creates relevant documents, of which the above-mentioned Strategy (EDS) is a pinnacle.

Provisions of international law and EU deal with norms referring to general principles in the field of public responsibility for social security of citizens, including groups that may experience social exclusion. The European law norms do not directly refer to the question of procedural guarantees, hence the lack of standards. The strategy (EDS) postulates changes in this respect, but in the mode of applying good practices and not harmonization (Mokrzycka 2012, p. 67). Thus, the role of good practices is huge, especially in view of the large variation in the application of legal instruments and procedures in individual countries. The possibility of identifying, indicating and formulating recommendations or guidelines based on good practice is becoming a significant condition for making changes in the quality of life of people with disabilities.

2 Employment of Disabled People in the Light of Statistics and Employment Support Models

There is a problem with obtaining methodologically homogeneous data on people with disabilities in the European Union countries, as well as in other national and international structures. The heterogeneity of data results from the lack of a universal concept and various definitions of disability in individual countries. This differentiation refers to both the definition of legal (registered) disability[2] and the definition of biological disability.[3] Data collection is an important and a very difficult task in the monitoring of the situation of people with disability and removing barriers that they face. The implementation of the Strategy (EDS 2010–2020) has brought some progress in the EU both in the collection of periodic disability statistics and the development of indicators to monitor the evolution of the situation (Commission Staff Working Document, Progress Report on the implementation of European Disability Strategy [2010–2020] 2017, p. 17). However, there are still methodological problems related to the comparability of data between individual countries.

Data on people who are legally certified to be disabled and are biologically disabled are collected as part of national censuses carried out at a certain frequency (in Poland every 10 years) and representative surveys (surveys): European Health Interview Survey (EHIS)[4] (every 5 years) and European Union Statistics on Income and Living Conditions (EU-SILC)[5] (every year). In the EU countries, a uniform definition of biological disability has been developed. In the collective statistics on disability of the European Union countries, usually the data presented refers to biological disability.[6] Data on legally disabled persons refer to the legal provisions in force in a given country regarding the determination of disability and therefore are not comparable for individual countries.

---

[2] Population of disabled persons, who have been defined on the basis of legal criterion, which consists of people who have a certificate of disability or inability to work.

[3] Population of persons, who declare that they have limitations in the performance of selected activities.

[4] https://ec.europa.eu/eurostat/statistics-explained/index.php/European_health_interview_survey_-_methodology.

[5] https://ec.europa.eu/eurostat/web/microdata/european-union-statistics-on-income-and-living-conditions.

[6] Disability measured through a concept of general activity limitation: "Limitation in activities people usually do because of health problems for at least the past six months" which is currently used in European Health Interview Survey (EHIS) and EU Statistics on Income and Living Conditions (EU-SILC). The indicator is based on data collected by the Global Activity Limitation Instrument (GALI): "For at least the past 6 months, to what extent have you been limited because of a health problem in activities people usually do? Would you say you have been … "severely limited/limited but not severely or/not limited at all?"", accessed: https://ec.europa.eu/eurostat/statistics-explained/index.php/Glossary:Disability, 7.1.2019.

Methodologically homogeneous data, based on the results of statistical surveys carried out in all European Community countries (in Poland conducted by the Central Statistical Office): EHIS and EU-SILC on the percentage share of people with disability (biologically disabled), are available on Eurostat's website (Statistical Office of the European Communities) for individual countries of the European Union. Such data are available on employed and unemployed people with disability.

In the case of providing data in the statistics of individual European Union countries, on the value of indicators of economic activity of disabled persons (activity rate, unemployment rate), the same definitions and the same methodology of their calculation are not always applied. The statistics are used from national censuses or the results of the study of economic activity of the population (Labour Force Survey LFS, BAEL in Poland). The reported statistics in national reports may differ from the data provided in the reports of international organisations of the EU (by Eurostat), OECD, ILO, WHO due to the different definition and classification of disabled people used to standardize data.

In order to supplement the information about people with disabilities, additional research is also carried out, such as the European health and social integration survey (EHSIS 2012), ad hoc module on employment in the labour force survey (LFS-AHM 2002 and 2011[7]). The results of this last study provide comparable data on the employment of people with disabilities. The situation of disabled people in individual EU countries on the labour market is diverse. People with long-term health or disability restrictions are much less active on the labour market than people without such restrictions (Fig. 1). The average employment rate for the EU was 38.7% (for non-disabled people 72.9%). Differences between countries are significant: the largest numbers of people with disability or health restrictions were employed in Sweden 64.0%, France 61.0%, Finland 51.4%, Luxemburg 49.8%, Austria 48.4%, the smallest in Bulgaria 18.0%, Hungary 18.4%, Ireland 22.0%, Romania 24.1% and Poland 26.7%. In all countries, the employment rates of men with

---

[7] The study uses the following definitions of disability: definition 1: People having a basic activity difficulty (such as sight, hearing, walking, communicating); definition 2: People limited in work because of a long-standing health problem and/or a basic activity difficulty (LHPAD), accessed: https://ec.europa.eu/eurostat/statistics-explained/index.php?title= Archive:Disability_statistics_-_labour_market_access, 7.1.2019.

health and disability-related restrictions are higher than those of women (Figs. 2 and 3). The age group 25–54 has the largest share in the labour market; age categories 15–24 and 55–64 have a significantly lower share. The average for the EU was: 15–24: 28.7%, 25–54: 48.8%, 55–64: 25.0% (Table 1).

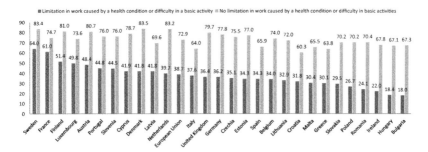

Fig. 1 Employment rate of people by type of disability in % (20–64), 2011 (*Source* European Commission: http://appsso.eurostat.ec.europa.eu/nui/show.do?dataset=hlth_dlm010&lang=en [accessed 14 January 2019])

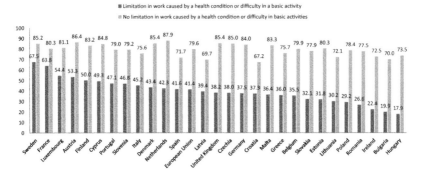

Fig. 2 Employment rate of people by type of disability in % (20–64), 2011 males (*Source* European Commission: http://appsso.eurostat.ec.europa.eu/nui/show.do?dataset=hlth_dlm010&lang=en [accessed 14 January 2019])

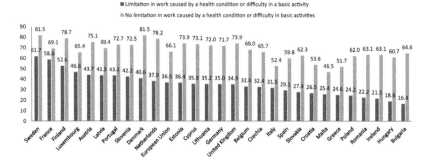

Fig. 3 Employment rate of people by type of disability in % (20–64), 2011 females (*Source* European Commission: http://appsso.eurostat.ec.europa.eu/nui/show.do?dataset=hlth_dlm010&lang=en [accessed 14 January 2019])

An indicator illustrating the disadvantageous situation of disabled people on the labour market is disability pay gap. This is the difference in the average remuneration of disabled and non-disabled people, expressed as a percentage. In the UK, where this type of statistics is collected, wage differentiation is an important issue in the public debate and an instrument that serves to mobilize employers to monitor the disability pay gap and solve the problems arising from these differences (TUC 2018). UK has a stable difference in the employment of people with disabilities and able-bodied workers (disability employment gap) of more than 30 percentage points. These values are not homogeneous for the entire population of disabled people. People with different impairments experience different levels of access to the job market. The pay gap between disabled and able-bodied people is also measured. The disability pay gap has multiple causes. Significant factors include: higher participation of disabled persons in part-time employment, in lower-wage occupations. Educational achievements are the driving force behind wage inequalities. Even when people with disabilities achieve comparable educational results with able-bodied people, they earn less. In this manner, discrimination against disabled people is holding back both educational achievement and progress once in work. Finally, women with disabilities face the most significant pay gaps, higher than those of men with disabilities (TUC 2018). Inequalities in the pay of disabled and able-bodied people are also to a certain extent the result of prejudices and discrimination in access to employment and in the workplace.

Table 1 Employment rate by type of disability by age in % (2011)

Country	Age	Limitation in work caused by a health condition or difficulty in a basic activity	No limitation in work caused by a health condition or difficulty in basic activities
European Union	15–24	28.7	33.6
European Union	25–54	48.8	80.9
European Union	55–64	25.0	54.5
Belgium	15–24	19.7	25.2
Belgium	25–54	43.7	85.6
Belgium	55–64	19.4	47.9
Bulgaria	15–24	–	22.5
Bulgaria	25–54	22.5	76.2
Bulgaria	55–64	14.9	53.1
Czech Republic	15–24	21.4	24.7
Czech Republic	25–54	44.3	86.1
Czech Republic	55–64	24.8	54.5
Denmark	15–24	41.4	60.2
Denmark	25–54	48.7	89.1
Denmark	55–64	28.2	71.6
Germany	15–24	37.0	42.4
Germany	25–54	43.8	83.6
Germany	55–64	25.6	66.2
Estonia	15–24	–	30.9
Estonia	25–54	41.9	82.9
Estonia	55–64	25.4	75.2
Ireland	15–24	13.6	29.9
Ireland	25–54	25.1	72.6
Ireland	55–64	17.6	58.0
Greece	15–24	–	16.7
Greece	25–54	37.3	71.7
Greece	55–64	24.3	46.1
Spain	15–24	18.1	24.3
Spain	25–54	43.8	71.6
Spain	55–64	20.4	53.6
France	15–24	33.7	30.1
France	25–54	70.0	85.9
France	55–64	40.9	48.0
Croatia	15–24	–	20.2
Croatia	25–54	41.3	72.4
Croatia	55–64	23.3	40.7
Italy	15–24	10.2	19.4
Italy	25–54	49.9	73.6
Italy	55–64	21.5	40.8
Cyprus	15–24	26.1	31.6

(continued)

Table 1 (continued)

Country	Age	Limitation in work caused by a health condition or difficulty in a basic activity	No limitation in work caused by a health condition or difficulty in basic activities
Cyprus	25–54	49.9	85.0
Cyprus	55–64	33.1	65.1
Latvia	15–24	–	25.7
Latvia	25–54	51.6	77.1
Latvia	55–64	31.0	57.8
Lithuania	15–24	–	18.4
Lithuania	25–54	39.5	81.6
Lithuania	55–64	26.0	59.7
Luxembourg	15–24	18.9	20.7
Luxembourg	25–54	63.8	84.9
Luxembourg	55–64	21.6	45.1
Hungary	15–24	–	18.4
Hungary	25–54	27.9	77.3
Hungary	55–64	10.6	46.8
Malta	15–24	–	42.1
Malta	25–54	42.0	74.3
Malta	55–64	18.4	35.1
Netherlands	15–24	39.8	64.9
Netherlands	25–54	46.8	89.4
Netherlands	55–64	28.0	65.1
Austria	15–24	52.1	53.2
Austria	25–54	66.6	88.4
Austria	55–64	24.7	49.9
Poland	15–24	13.2	25.8
Poland	25–54	38.2	81.2
Poland	55–64	17.1	45.0
Portugal	15–24	18.4	27.6
Portugal	25–54	54.7	83.1
Portugal	55–64	33.4	58.5
Romania	15–24	–	25.1
Romania	25–54	32.4	79.5
Romania	55–64	19.0	53.9
Slovenia	15–24	30	31.0
Slovenia	25–54	64.9	87.5
Slovenia	55–64	19.1	41.3
Slovakia	15–24	19.3	20.6
Slovakia	25–54	40.7	80.3
Slovakia	55–64	16.9	51.4
Finland	15–24	37.8	41.5
Finland	25–54	66.1	86.6

(continued)

Table 1 (continued)

Country	Age	Limitation in work caused by a health condition or difficulty in a basic activity	No limitation in work caused by a health condition or difficulty in basic activities
Finland	55–64	34.0	71.5
Sweden	15–24	35.4	41.2
Sweden	25–54	68.7	89.1
Sweden	55–64	57.4	77.5
United Kingdom	15–24	32.3	52.4
United Kingdom	25–54	42.2	85.3
United Kingdom	55–64	26.5	66.4

Source European Commission: http://appsso.eurostat.ec.europa.eu/nui/show.do?dataset=hlth_dlm01 0&lang=en (accessed 14 January 2019)

Regardless of the accepted concept and definition of disability, statistics regarding the employment of people with disabilities and their working conditions show that their employment rate and pay are below the values in the able-bodied population. This is a worrying phenomenon because in the light of the World Health Organization projections, the number of disabled people is constantly growing, due to the ageing of the population and the increased risk of disability in the elderly. There is also a global trend of increasing incidence of chronic diseases that cause disability, such as diabetes, cardiovascular disease or mental illness. Environmental and other factors present in individual countries such as transport, road accidents, natural disasters, conflicts, diets, abuse of psychoactive substances also affect disability growth (WHO 2011, p. 260). The cited report stressed that although the majority of people with disabilities at productive age could be productive, employment rates are much lower and unemployment rates higher than in the group of able-bodied people. It is influenced by many factors, including: lack of access to education, rehabilitation and vocational training, lack of access to finance for establishing and running one's own business, construction of disability benefits system in a manner that discourages work, unavailability of workplaces and perception of disability and the disabled by employers (WHO 2011, p. 250).

The international organisations among others (UN, ILO, Council of Europe, EU) and national stakeholders, including the government, local government institutions, employers, organisations of disabled people, trade unions, and others working towards increasing the opportunities of disabled persons on the labour market, play an important role. One of the ways of combating the exclusion of disabled people from the labour market lies in designing and implementing various programmes in the field of activation and employment, including special systems, preferring the employment of disabled people, on the open labour market. In activities aimed at increasing the employment of disabled persons on the open labour market, a special place is attributed to employers, on whose attitudes and involvement jobs for people with disabilities depend (Garbat 2012, p. 123). Employers are provided with various incentives to encourage or even enforce employment for disabled people.

In Europe, there are various systems of professional activation and employment support for people with disabilities, addressed to employers. The two most commonly used are:

1. Quota system (redistributive, share),
2. System based on civic rights (anti-discrimination, libertarian).

The quota model (also called share model) assumes the necessity to take into account higher labour costs of disabled people (generated, e.g., by adjusting workplaces to their needs), which may discourage employers from employing such people (Jaworski 2009, pp. 34–35).

Therefore, states impose on employers a statutory obligation to employ people with disabilities as a certain percentage of the workforce in relation to employees who are able-bodied. Because this obligation is ubiquitous, all employers are at risk of higher costs of employing people with disabilities, while those who do not employ them pay a special fee for not fulfilling their obligation. In this model, there is a redistribution of funds from employers not employing people with disabilities to those employing more than the required minimum. The latter usually receive certain subsidies for jobs created for people with disabilities. The share model therefore has a strict separation of the labour market for able-bodied and disabled people. Such a model exists in, among others, post-communist countries (e.g. in Poland), but also in France and Germany.

The anti-discrimination model, also known as libertarian model is applied in wealthier countries (e.g. UK, Sweden, Ireland and the United States). It is based on the assumption of equal access to the labour market for people with disabilities and those without disabilities on the basis of the exercise of their citizens' rights. There is no statutory obligation to employ people with disabilities. It is also accepted that there is no need to create separate regulations on the employment of disabled persons. What is more, such regulations can be interpreted as based on mercy and denying the idea of equality and equal opportunities. Persons with disabilities should receive work on the so-called open labour market. An important role is played by all educational activities, encouraging employees with disabilities to enter the labour market, and employers to employ them (Jaworski 2009, pp. 33–34).

The quota system is much more popular and is usually applied to employers from the private and public sectors.

According to ILO/OECD estimates, it occurs in over 50 countries around the world. In some countries using a quota-levy system, which requires companies to pay a levy if they don't meet the established quota, there is also the option to meet the quota by to buying goods and services from sheltered workshops or other companies, which employ a significant number of disabled employees (ILO/OECD 2018, p. 14). Quota systems are diverse and constantly reformed at the level of individual countries. They have many varieties. In Europe, the obligatory employment rate for disabled people, in countries applying the quota system, ranges from 4 to 8% (Garbat 2012, p. 516). However, it should be emphasized that both systems, anti-discrimination legislation and employment quota, can be used in a complementary fashion and many countries use both.

The search for more effective and efficient systems of professional activation and supporting the employment of disabled people on the open labour market favours various modifications of support models and hybrid solutions (combining elements of the quota and anti-discrimination system) or developing own solutions at the level of individual countries.

Denmark is an example. There a new model of the labour market was introduced, defined as flexicurity combining a flexible labour market with social security and active labour market policy (Wilthagen and Tros 2004). The essence of the Danish labour market is the freedom of employers to dismiss and hire employees, but it is combined with guarantees of support for people losing employment. The responsibilities of public administration and self-government authorities in relation to the creation and implementation of policies on local labour markets have been strengthened, because the integration of disabled people is a duty of public authorities and is not shared with individual employers. The system of supporting the employment of people with disabilities in

Denmark is based on motivating employers to hire disabled people, by appealing to the public opinion. There are no sanctions or penalties for employers for not hiring people with disabilities. The support system is based on their voluntary participation, and the identification and promotion of employers applying good practices in society (Garbat 2012: 120). Economic incentives (e.g. wage subsidies prompt employers to employ work-disabled people, Høgelund 2003, p. 106) and moral suasion play a role. Moral arguments are used in government campaigns for the social responsibility of employers in integrating disabled people into the labour market. Local Coordination Committees are in operation. Their goal is to involve employers and other participants in disability policy. They also use elements of moral persuasion and information (Høgelund 2003, p. 106).

The comparison of the Danish model and the quota model indicates the importance of the balance between the obligations and privileges granted by public authorities to employers employing people with disabilities: "[...] an optimal disability policy neither should demand too little nor too much of employers, whose cooperation is after all a precondition for the integration of disabled people. It might therefore be worth considering this aspect when nations consider reforming their disability policies in order to meet future welfare state pressures" (Høgelund 2003, p. 177). In this situation, the role of good practices, encouraging employers to create efficient work environments that draw on the potential of human diversity, is becoming increasingly important at the national and international levels.

In the literature on the subject, there is also a new system called disability benchmarking. This system was created in the last decade of the twentieth century in the United States and consists of determining the proportion of disabled workers who have to be employed in a company, if the company is to be permitted to participate in government contracts. It is not an obligation imposed on employers (as in the standard quota system), but a condition of participation in this segment of the public procurement market. At the same time, it should be emphasized that disability benchmarking is related to disability management in the workplace. It is an introduction to the area of current management of such solutions that are conducive to employing people with various disabilities (Piotrowska 2015).

The objective of the existing and constantly reformed systems of vocational activation and support of employment discussed above is to help people with disabilities find employment and to stay employed, by making employers from the open labour market more active in this direction. Debates on existing support systems and their effectiveness prompt one to take into account many factors: legal traditions, political, cultural and socio-economic conditions (Sargeant et al. 2016). This problem is addressed by the aforementioned researchers analysing support systems in Italy, Russia and the UK.

Quota systems exist in most EU countries and in many other countries around the world, but according to the WHO, "the assumption that quotas correct labour market imperfections to the benefit of persons with disabilities is yet to be documented empirically, as no thorough impact evaluation of quotas on employment of persons with disabilities has been performed" (WHO 2011, pp. 241–242). In the EU, there is also a directive on equal treatment in employment and occupation (Council Directive 2000/78/EC of 27 November 2000 establishing a general framework for equal treatment in employment and occupation), which aims to achieve equality in employment and freedom from discrimination (including in relation to disability). In many EU countries, anti-discrimination legislation is in force along with a quota policy and one cannot really say which one is more effective. For example, the UK has no worse data on the employment of people with disabilities, although it uses only one of these two systems (it withdrew from the quota system and applies an anti-discrimination system). According to the ILO, there is evidence that legislation requiring quotas for disabled workers can act as a catalyst for employers, a factor accelerating changes in the policy on the recruitment and retention of people with disabilities (ILO 2007/2014, p. 58). On the other hand, quota regulations, in the countries in which they are effective, pose a risk of undermining the idea that people with disabilities should be employed for the same reasons as non-disabled people, that is, because of their skills and talent. Employment of people because of their disability in order to avoid fees and sanctions provided for in the regulations governing the quota system may induce employers to treat disabled workers differently than those who are able-bodied, for example, by offering them fewer career opportunities (ILO 2014, p. 11).

As emphasized by the authors of the analysis mentioned (Sargeant et al. 2016), the problem with quota systems is that sends a mixed message to both employers and people with disabilities. On the one hand, it is said that the employment of people with disabilities is desirable, and on the other, this message implies that workers with disabilities are not able to compete on equal footing on the open labour market. The quota system is based on the medical approach, as well as obligations and sanctions.

This means that a disabled person is treated mainly as a problem and not as a potential resource as other employees. Thus, employers often employ people with disabilities only to meet legal requirements. The authors of the report conclude that quota systems may contribute to increasing the participation of disabled people in the labour market (but require support from other factors and policies affecting the labour market), while anti-discrimination policy seems more appropriate for the normalization principle. It favours the implementation of the principle of equal opportunities in society, through the promotion of employers' initiatives and the change of social awareness (Sargeant et al. 2016).

Measures aimed at changing social attitudes and awareness of employers as an opportunity to improve the employment rate of people with disabilities are promoted in many studies. The WHO report emphasized that many of the interventions made on the labour market are not successful; hence, the growing impact of factors aimed at providing knowledge and changing the attitudes of employers and employees of HR departments and disseminating good, model organisational practices (WHO 2011, pp. 251–252). There is a lot of evidence that employers employing people with disabilities are more likely to hire new employees with disabilities and are open to innovative activities in this area (Cascio and Boudreau 2010; Gąciarz and Giermanowska 2009). The role of information campaigns in implementing the law promoting the employment of disabled persons and encouraging the implementation of good employment practices is emphasized. Information campaigns may refer to the rights and obligations of disabled persons and employers, introduced regulations, the scope of services and employment support measures (ILO 2007/2014, p. 59). The effectiveness of legislation and policies aimed at promoting equal employment for disabled people depends on the implementation of the measures in practice.

3 Determinants of the Employment Policy of Disabled People as a Public Policy

The employment policy of people with disabilities as any public policy is determined by many factors of varying complexity. The content and scope of implemented solutions in the area of a given public policy and their implementation method depend on various conditions. The term can be understood both as existing international and national regulations and sociocultural and economic phenomena and processes whose occurrence, scale and intensity affect the possibility of applying specific instruments, purposeful changes and their implementations. Some researchers consider them as independent variables, which should be identified, analysed, predicted and taken into account in the development of strategies dealing with change (Żołędowski 2007, p. 56). Such conditions may include (cf. Żołędowski 2007, pp. 59–60):

- Political conditions, related to political doctrine, affecting the organisation of the administration and the political situation of a given state;
- Economic conditions related to the economic development of a given country and the related situation on the labour market;
- Conditions related to human resources associated with demographic processes, shaping the structure of the population (in terms of quantitative labour resources) and sociocultural processes shaping the social structure (in relation to human and social capital);
- Conditions related to the existing public policy model that determines the scope of the introduced changes either through small evolutionary improvements of public policy tools or through thorough reforms, as was the case in the countries of Central and Eastern Europe;
- External conditions, they are related to both spontaneous social processes, and also those resulting from the membership of a given country of international structures and community organisations.

With regard to the employment policy for people with disabilities, some conditions have already been mentioned, such as international UN and ILO regulations and EU recommendations affecting national legal and procedural standards and social practices. These are important external conditions, the significance of which will grow. In the last two decades, researchers have increasingly described contemporary social policy or public policies as intergovernmental and/or supranational than national (see Deacon et al. 1997). The term "intergovernmental" means the form of decision-making in many international organisations, e.g. the ILO, when the structure of authoritative decision-making enjoying external and internal sovereignty (Kennett 2001, p. 31).

Supranational governance refers to supranational rules, institutions and practices that are beyond the control of one state, as evidenced by the EU. This does not mean that researchers abandoned comparative analyses. Patricia Kennett even argues that (2001, p. 38) "Cross-national social policy analysis is not only an appropriate strategy, but also a vital one for understanding the complexity of contemporary social change". We present below the typology of disability policy models, based on the diversity of the axiological assumptions of social policy that affect the selection of practical tools. Like Patricia Kennett, we believe that such studies can highlight the diversity and differences between nation states. "It is vital then that the researcher does not assume a 'value-consensus' across societies and recognizes that concepts and their meanings are dynamic and change over time" (Kennett 2001, p. 46). They also help to avoid the mistake of irreflective transfer of good practices without taking into the account existing institutional and social conditions.

Existing typologies of disability policy models refer to the models of welfare regimes described by Esping-Andersen in 1990. They draw attention to historical ways of shaping social policy models, including disability policy. They indicate the importance of internal conditions related to the existing model. The following groups of countries and models in OECD countries are distinguished (OECD 2010, p. 88):

1. "Social democratic" model (mostly north European countries): sub-group A (Denmark, Netherlands, Switzerland), sub-group B (Finland, Germany, Norway, Sweden);
2. "Liberal" model (OECD Pacific and English-speaking countries): sub-group A (Australia, New Zealand, UK), sub-group B (Canada, Japan, Korea, the United States);
3. "Corporatist" model (mostly continental European countries): sub-group A (Austria, Belgium, Hungary), sub-group B (France, Greece, Luxembourg, Poland), sub-group C (Czech Republic, Ireland, Italy, Portugal, Slovak Republic, Spain).

The social-democratic disability policy model is characterized by a relatively generous and accessible compensation policy package, a low entry threshold for a partial disability benefit and generous sickness and disability benefits (OECD 2010, p. 89). This model ensures a broad and equally accessible integration policy package, with particularly strong focus on vocational rehabilitation. This policy is expensive, but it provides good support to people who can and want to work. There are two variants of this model. One group, including Denmark, Switzerland and the Netherlands, have less generous benefits and employment support than other countries, but they provide better work and incentives. Germany and countries belonging to the Scandinavian model Finland, Sweden and Norway have the most generous benefit and support systems (with full population coverage, low entry thresholds, high benefits, vocational rehabilitation programmes) in the OECD countries. However, they introduce the strongest obligations for employers.

The Liberal disability policy model is characterized by a much less generous compensation policy setup, with lower benefit levels and a much higher threshold to get onto benefits (OECD 2010, p. 89). Monitoring the presence of people with disabilities in the labour market is not well developed. Employment and vocational rehabilitation policies are relatively underdeveloped. In contrast, incentives to work are strong, and the rules of suspension of benefits are very flexible. This configuration of the support policy is less expensive. This model also includes two variants. The countries of the group including Australia, New Zealand and the UK have much better organized, coordinated and accessible services. The second group covering Canada, the United States, Japan and Korea have the most stringent eligibility criteria for becoming legally disabled and full disability benefits.

The Corporatist disability policy model can be interpreted as intermediate, relative to the other two models. Benefits are relatively accessible and relatively generous, employment programmes are quite developed, but not on the level of the Nordic model. This model is characterized by a smaller range of measures, a limited number of benefits and incentives to work.

The Corporatist model covers a large number of countries mostly in the south, east and west of Europe. This model also includes three variants. The countries of the first group, including Austria, Belgium and Hungary, are distinguished by a good development of rehabilitation programmes, as well as employment programmes combined with lower levels of benefits and a stronger employment orientation. The countries from the second subgroup France, Greece, Luxembourg and Poland pay the most generous sickness and disability benefits among the group of countries from this model. They focus on temporary disability benefits; there is more attention to sickness absence monitoring and a lack of benefit suspension possibilities. The third group, comprising the Czech Republic, Ireland, Italy, Portugal, the Slovak Republic and Spain, have relatively underdeveloped employment and rehabilitation policies. The level of sickness benefits is lower than in other subgroups of this model, but the periods of receiving sickness benefits are longer (OECD 2010, pp. 89–90).

Models of disability policy remained distinct, but they are more similar now than some 15–20 years ago (OECD 2010, p. 91). This is due to policy changes in relation to incapacity benefits, including reducing the dependence of disabled persons on the benefits system and increasing support related to employment of disabled persons. In many countries, the so-called redistributive policies (based on schemes for income maintenance) have been criticized from the beginning of the twenty-first century as being too expensive and deactivating people with disabilities (Hvinden and Halvorsen 2003). In addition, there were critical analyses regarding the quality and scale of social services offered to disabled people, especially in relation to rehabilitation and vocational activation services. The imbalance in the overall policy effort in disability area was also highlighted. "In particular, it has been argued that in practice too much emphasis has been put on administrating particular schemes for income maintenances or services for people with impairment. At the same time the policy efforts to remove barriers against equal participation in society and work have been insufficient and weak" (Hvinden and Halvorsen 2003, p. 303). There has been a clear trend and grass-roots pressure to create the so-called disability policy of regulation, related to the emerging from the end of the 1980s European Union strategy to combat discrimination and promote equal opportunities for all citizens. The policy model based on civic rights emphasizes the need to implement the principles of universal design and anti-discrimination provisions and actions. The principle of non-discrimination refers in particular to the issue of employment, including the recruitment and retention of an employee with disability. The challenge for European disability policy and national-level policies will be introducing a balance between redistributive types of disability provisions and the implementation of regulatory type of disability policies, based on non-discrimination and universal design.

In earlier sections, we also pointed to global changes concerning expectations of disabled people, articulated through social movements for their emancipation. The result of these pressures is a change in the paradigm of defining and perceiving the phenomenon of disability (social model). This is synthetically described by Dan Goodley (2011, pp. 3–4), who stresses the contribution of the social movements of people with disabilities in creating politics at (inter) national level and building national and supranational organisations. These are also a kind of external conditions affecting the social expectations in a given country under the influence of already existing changes in other countries.

The impact described above, of external conditions based on legal-procedural, institutional and sociocultural contexts and internal factors, linked with the existing model of public policy, is particularly visible in countries undergoing fundamental political system changes, which join the international communities on the principle of a "late arrival". At the same time, in these countries, the impact of existing well-established bureaucratic practices and social institutions on new solutions is also revealed. An example is Poland, whose disability policy illustrates "multidimensional incoherence" (Gąciarz 2017, p. 85). "Multidimensional incoherence" is the result of the occurrence of conflicting concepts resulting from axiologically different assumptions about the functions and tasks of the welfare state. On the one hand, it is considered necessary and right to conduct a policy of activation and social integration of disabled people, which results from efforts for political correctness and conformism towards the EU structures (or the Council of Europe) and the expectations of the community of people with disabilities. On the other hand, there is still the policy of compensation and securing the needs of people with disabilities at the minimum level (Gąciarz 2017, p. 85). There are also pilot projects, implemented from European funds, but they have local coverage and there are obstacles to their dissemination, whereas local conditions and the environmental dimension play a very important role in improving the living conditions of people with disabilities.

Also in countries with more advanced economic growth under capitalist conditions and a well-established democratic system, the implementation of a social model based on human rights may prove difficult in the face of long-standing social practices that are associated with the existing social security model. James G. Rice (2009) on the example of Iceland shows how deeply rooted is the medical understanding of disability in the routine activities of social services and how it affects the social perception of disabled pensioners. This everyday operationalization of the definition of disability in practice determines the advancement of the implementation of the social model.

Research reports also identify the conditions for employing people with disabilities related to local labour resources in local and regional terms in relation to single countries. They are particularly interesting when the political system of the country and its territorial organisation assume independence in running regional policies, as in the United States. The analysis conducted for the United States showed the existing—albeit small—impact of political and economic conditions on the scale of employment of disabled people at the local level (Sevak et al. 2016). However, a greater impact was noted for environmental conditions, i.e. due to the socio-physical features of the residential environment of disabled people. Research conducted has shown that inhabiting metropolitan and urban areas, where there are facilities in the form of urban transport and there is access to doctors, does not clearly affect the employment rate of disabled people. However, the importance of sociocultural norms in a given community and individual characteristics of people with disabilities in relation to employment was confirmed. Living in a community that shares the norms of work and participating in the social division of labour increases the employment rate of people with disabilities. In addition, the importance of factors related to health and individual characteristics was emphasized. With regard to political and economic determinants, the authors called for further research that "should examine whether economic conditions, policies, and other features of the environment may matter more for some subgroups or individuals than they do for others" (Sevak et al. 2016, p. 17).

REFERENCES

Cascio, Wayne, and John Boudreau. 2010. *Investing in People: Financial Impact of Human Resource Initiatives*. Upper Saddle River, NJ: FT Press.

Commission Staff Working Document. 2017. *Progress Report on the Implementation of the European Disability Strategy (2010–2020)*. Brussels, 2.2.2017 SWD, 29 Final.

Convention on the Rights of Persons with Disabilities (CRPD) and Optional Protocol. 2006. http://www.un.org/disabilities/documents/convention/convoptprot-e.pdf.

Cotter, Anne M. 2007. *This Ability: An International Legal Analysis of Disability Discrimination*. Aldershot, Hampshire: Ashgate.

Council Directive 2000/78/EC of 27 November 2000 Establishing a General Framework for Equal Treatment in Employment and Occupation.

Deacon, Bob, Michelle Hulse, and Paul Stubbs. 1997. *Global Social Policy: International Organizations and the Future of Welfare*. London: Sage.

Dunay, Anna, Ambuj Sharma, and Csaba Bálint Illés. 2016. "Disability and Employment—An Overview on the Role of Education and Educators." Conference Paper, October 2016.
European Disability Strategy 2010–2020: A Renewed Commitment to a Barrier-Free Europe /* COM/2010/0636 Final */. Accessed https://eur-lex.europa.eu/legal-content/EN/TXT/?uri=celex:52010DC0636.
Gąciarz, Barbara, and Ewa Giermanowska, eds. 2009. *Zatrudniając niepełnosprawnych. Wiedza, opinie i doświadczenia pracodawców*. Warszawa: Fundacja Instytut Spraw Publicznych.
Gąciarz, Barbara. 2017. "Polityka społeczna wobec niepełnosprawności. Zarządzanie problemem czy strategia empowerment?" In *Niezatrudnieniowe wymiary aktywizacji. W stronę modelu empowerment?* edited by Arkadiusz Karwacki, Marek Rymsza, Barbara Gąciarz, Tomasz Kaźmierczak, and Bohdan Skrzypczak, 63–105. Toruń: Wydawnictwo UMK.
Garbat, Marcin. 2012. *Zatrudnianie i rehabilitacja zawodowa osób z niepełnosprawnością w Europie*. Zielona Góra: Oficyna Wydawnicza Uniwersytetu Zielonogórskiego.
Goodley, Dan. 2011. *Disability Studies: An Interdisciplinary Introduction*. London: Sage.
Høgelund, Jan. 2003. *In Search of Effective Disability Policy: Comparing the Developments and Outcomes of the Dutch and Danish Disability Policies*. Amsterdam: Amsterdam University Press.
Hvinden, Bjørn, and Rune Halvorsen. 2003. "Which Way for European Disability Policy?" *Scandinavian Journal of Disability Research* 5 (3): 296–312.
ILO/OECD. 2018. "Labour Market Inclusion of People with Disabilities." Paper Presented at the 1st Meeting of the G20 Employment Working Group 20–22 February 2018, Buenos Aires, Argentina.
ILO. 2014. *Business as Unusual: Making Workplaces Inclusive of People with Disabilities*. Geneva.
ILO. 2007/2014. *Achieving Equal Employment Opportunities for People with Disabilities Through Legislation*. Geneva.
Jaworski, Jacek. 2009. *Praca dla osób niepełnosprawnych w zwalczaniu ich wykluczenia społecznego. Ocena polskiego systemu wspierania zatrudnienia osób niepełnosprawnych*. Warsaw: IPiSS.
Kennett, Patricia. 2001. *Comparative Social Policy: Theory and Research*. Buckingham and Philadelphia: Open University Press.
Kurowski, Krzysztof. 2014. *Wolności i prawa człowieka i obywatela z perspektywy osób z niepełnosprawnościami*. Warsaw: Biuletyn Rzecznika Praw Obywatelskich [Ombudsman Bulletin].
Mikołajczyk-Lerman, Grażyna. 2013. *Między wykluczeniem a integracją – realizacja praw dziecka niepełnosprawnego i jego rodziny*. Łódź: Wydawnictwo Uniwersytetu Łódzkiego.

Mokrzycka, Anna. 2012. "Europejskie podejście do praw osób niepełnosprawnych w świetle regulacji. Znaczenie Disability Action Plan oraz European Disability Strategy 2010-2020." *Polityka Społeczna*, pp. 61-70.
OECD. 2010. *Sickness, Disability and Work: Breaking the Barriers.*
Oliver, Michael. 1990. *The Politics of Disablement.* London: Macmillan.
Oliver, Michael. 2009. *Understanding Disability: From Theory to Practice.* Basingstoke: Palgrave Macmillan.
Piotrowska, Dorota. 2015. "Zespoły zróżnicowane pod kątem sprawności." *Personel* 4: 18-22.
Rembis, Michael. 2010/2015. "Disability Studies." In *International Encyclopedia of Rehabilitation*, edited by John H. Stone and Michael Blouin. Buffalo: Center for International Rehabilitation Research Information and Exchange, 2010; Revised 2015. http://cirrie.buffalo.edu/encyclopedia/article.php?id=281&language=en. Accessed September 26, 2018.
Rembis, Michael, and Natalia Pamuła. 2016. "Disability Studies: A View from Humanities." *Człowiek-Niepełnosprawność -Społeczeństwo* 1 (31): 5-23.
Rice, James G. 2009. "The Operationalization of Disability in Policy and Practice." In *Rannsóknir í félagsvísindum x félags- og mannvísindadeild. Erindi flutt á ráðstefnu í október 2009*, edited by Gunnar Þór Jóhannessonog and Helga Björnsdóttir, 263-272. Reykjavík: Félagsvísindastofnun Háskóla Íslands.
Sargeant, Malcolm, Elena Radevich-Katsaroumpa, and Alessandra Innesti. 2016. "Disability Quotas: Past or Future Policy?" https://doi.org/10.1177/0143831X16639655. https://journals.sagepub.com/toc/eida/39/3. First Published April 6, 2016: 404-421.
Sevak, Purvi, John O'Neill, Andrew J. Houtenville, and Debra L. Brucker. 2016. "State and Local Determinants of Employment Outcomes Among Individuals with Disabilities." US Census Bureau Center for Economic Studies Paper No. CES-WP-16-21.
Sullivan, Kathryn. 2011. "The Prevalence of the Medical Model of Disability in Society." AHS Capstone Projects, Paper 13.
TUC. 2018. "Disability Employment and Pay Gaps 2018." https://www.tuc.org.uk/sites/default/files/Disabilityemploymentandpaygaps.pdf. Accessed February 1, 2019.
Wilthagen, Ton, and Frank Tros. 2004. "The Concepts of 'Flexicurity': A New Approach to Regulating Employment and Labour Markets." *Transfer* 10 (2): 166-186.
WHO. 2011. "World Report on Disability 2011."
Żołędowski, Cezary. 2007. "Uwarunkowania polityki społecznej." In *Polityka społeczna. Podręcznik akademicki*, edited by Grażyna Firlit-Fesnak and Małgorzata Szylko-Skoczny, 55-70. Warsaw: Wydawnictwo Naukowe PWN.

CHAPTER 3

Multivariate Conditions of Introducing People with Disabilities to the Labour Market: Coupled Impact and the Effect of Synergy

Abstract In the previous chapter, we discussed the importance of major international documents for creating conditions conductive to the employment of people with disabilities and running a new type of public disability policy at national level. In this chapter, we want to identify and discuss the bundles of factors affecting the employment of people with disabilities by companies and public institutions on domestic and local labour markets. We identify these factors in the subsystems of law, economy, society and culture, and organisational level of enterprises or labour market institutions (public/non-public). In our opinion, the effect of employment for people with disabilities is a result of the synergy of all the factors.

Keywords Models of disability · ICIDH and ICF conceptualizations · Assistive technologies · Factors of activity of people with disabilities on the labour market · "Bundle of factors" model

1 THE HISTORY OF SANCTIONING NON-EMPLOYMENT OF PEOPLE WITH DISABILITIES

1.1 The Real Nature of Disability and Its Determinants

The position of people with disabilities in the history of societies has always been special and generally associated with a sense of otherness, and often isolation and exclusion. Ronald J. Berger claims that

"Disability is a social enigma. Throughout history people have felt compelled both to stare at the disabled people in their midst and then to turn their heads in discomfort" (Berger 2013, p. 1). Colin Barnes and Geof Mercer emphasize that the location of disabled people on the "inferior" side of social division resulted from moving them from the public to the private sphere of life. The marginalization of people with disabilities has intensified with the development of industrial capitalism. This has led to an unfavourable financial situation, powerlessness and demeaning cultural stereotypes (Barnes and Mercer 2003).

Vic Finkelstein (1980) believes that manifestations of attitudes and practices towards people with disabilities are culturally conditioned and according to him have different forms depending on the phase of economic and technological development: pre-industrial (feudal society), industrial capitalism and post-industrial society. In the pre-industrial period, the agrarian society and work in rural households prevailed. People with disabilities occupied a low position in the social hierarchy, but they were expected to participate in economic activities. Depending on the type of disease or disability, they were included in social life. The degree of marginalization and support from the community was varied. There was social acceptance for people unable to work and without a source of livelihood to live off begging and alms. In this manner, the term "handicap" was born, which in its original meaning referred to disabled people supporting themselves on alms. The term composing of two words: hand and cap defines itself (Garbat 2012, p. 72).

The second phase analysed by Finkelstein (1980) is related to the emergence of industrial capitalism in nineteenth-century Europe and North America. The spread of free-market economy, paid work and mechanized production systems resulted in the accumulation of restrictions on the work of people with disabilities. This led to the removal of disabled workers from workplaces as "unproductive" people. People with disabilities have been removed from the mainstream of economic activity and directed to the market of other, marginal activities such as: cottage industry, handicrafts and street trade. In the era of industrial capitalism, there was a qualitative change in the social response to impairment that Mike Oliver (1990) called the social creation of disability as a personal tragedy.

This change had its source in the medical approach to the phenomenon of disability and the establishment of the medical model as the dominant one in the formulation of disability policy for over a century (Myhill and Blanck 2009). This approach, on the one hand, helped to change the situation of people with disabilities. These people were considered worthy of diagnosis and medical treatment and perceived more kindly in society. However, kindness was often a result of pity, and people with disabilities were still stigmatized and perceived "as less than full human beings" (Berger 2013, p. 2).

The basic assumption of this approach, referred to as the medical model, as we pointed out in the first chapter, is that disability results from the physical or mental limitations of the individual and is largely unrelated to the physical and social environment in which people live.

Because disability is treated as a matter of health or rehabilitation, the first step is to heal or find a cure for the disability. If this fails, the government and the public should focus on providing care and services to support the disabled (Myhill and Blanck 2009). This is crucial in approaching work and formulating employment policy goals for people with disabilities. Due to the emphasis placed on the model of medical care for people with disabilities, people with disabilities may be exempted from normal social duties "such *as work, and institutionalization and segregation are ultimately given justification*" (Gottlieb et al. 2010, p. 2, but see also Blanck 2008). This approach has a negative impact on the employment performance of people with disabilities, because it limits their ability to make choices, to be economically self-sufficient and to reach their full professional potential. It strengthens existing prejudices among employers regarding inability of disabled people to perform work, as well as apprehension of disabled people themselves (Shapiro 1994). This has important implications for people with disabilities and decision-makers. In countries where the medical model of disability is applied, people with disabilities are rarely employed, and when they are employed, they are usually in isolated workplaces (Lunt and Thornton 1994). The medical model of disability perpetuates protected or segregated employment opportunities that are not part of an open labour market (Shapiro 1994; Gottlieb et al. 2010).

The third phase of development according to Finkelstein (1980) is the post-industrial society that emerged in the second half of the twentieth century. This is the phase of computerized information technology, which is a harbinger of economic and social changes. Manuel Castells, describing the changes taking place in capitalist societies since the 1990s, calls them "network societies" (Castells 1996). New technologies, thanks to technical and communication solutions, have created previously impossible opportunities on the labour market for people with disabilities, new opportunities to take up paid work and thus lead an independent life. On the other hand, the literature on the subject emphasizes that not all the consequences of the new information economy are recognized, and that it may have beneficial as well as negative effects (Barnes and Mercer 2003).

Assistive technologies (AT) play an increasing role in improving the functional capabilities of people with disabilities. Some of them are relatively little technically advanced and very well known, such as reading glasses, crutches and hearing aids. Others more advanced, relying on the latest science and technology, can have a huge impact on the lives of people with disabilities. However, their use, as shown by the results of the project devoted to the role of AT in building the inclusive environment of people with disabilities, must take into account a number of conditions (*Assistive Technologies for People with Disabilities* 2018). Researchers working on the use of AT noted inequalities in the use of technologies in the divided European societies. Social and economic divisions exist in European societies. There are differences between those who can afford private health care and use AT outside the welfare state and those who have limited access. While public health care is still offered, it is not always sufficient for everyone in need, moreover, many AT are only available on the private market. This means that access to AT depends on the individual economic position, and many people with disabilities do not have access to them.

It is also worth emphasizing that technology alone is not enough to change the functioning of people with disabilities in society, education and employment. In research dealing with the workplace, several ATs have been identified that can support people with disabilities to provide them with employment and to pursue a career. However, this does not mean a full inclusion. Problems of discrimination and stigmatization may still occur. This requires broad actions directed not only to people with disabilities, but also introducing organisational changes, such as solutions related to flexible working time or teleworking (*Assistive Technologies for People with Disabilities* 2018).

Relations between people and technology must be understood in a wider social, historical and cultural context and take into account the accessibility for all users. Communication technologies and new media provide greater and faster access to education, trade, employment and entertainment, overcome barriers and increase access for people with disabilities. However, modern technologies can create unexpected and under-critiqued forms of social exclusion for disabled people. Hence, there are proposals for alternative thinking about technology as inclusive and accessible as opposed to assistive technology. "Accessible technologies would not be seen as are placement for, but rather a way to augment brick and mortar accessibility, thereby creating multiple points of access for all users. This approach would consider the needs of those with cognitive, sensory and physical disabilities as important sources of diversity and complexity necessary to inform the design of technology to increase accessibility and usability for all users" (Foley and Ferri 2012, p. 199).

Developed by researchers with a materialistic attitude (including Finkelstein, Oliver, Barnes and Mercer), "thesis on industrialization" and its impact on creating a modern Western definition of "disability" (as a separate social category and experience) is widely shared in many studies. It allows us to understand a wide range of disability relations, paying attention to the structural basis of the experiences of people with disabilities and showing how disability is created. The analytical value of the thesis on industrialization suggests the importance of changing material conditions and how this affected the lives of people with disabilities in history, e.g. barriers to paid employment as well as accessibility of the built environment have a significant impact on the position of people with disability in society (Turner and Blackie 2018). Approaches related to the removal of various types of barriers occurring in societies, have gained wide publicity and acceptance of disabled people's movements, and are developed using contemporary concepts (models) referring to the phenomenon of disability.

The following phases of development of the societies of Western civilization were accompanied by changes in the approach to the phenomenon of disability and legal regulations concerning defining disability and rights of disabled persons, including the right to work. The second important model of disability, following the medical model, is the social model of disability, which recognizes disability as a consequence of environmental and social barriers and attitudes that prevent disabled people from participating in society. This model had a positive impact on employment of disabled people in the United States, Canada and Australia. These people gained individualized and competitive employment in the community, and this approach helped change the negative attitude that employers may have towards people with disabilities (Shapiro 1994; Gottlieb et al. 2010).

The third model, a biopsychosocial model adopted by the World Health Organization (WHO), provides a framework that integrates medical and social disability models. WHO (2001) found that neither the medical model nor the social model of disability are in themselves sufficient to fully understand or reduce disability, although each of them has clear strengths. In the biopsychosocial model, which we have already mentioned in the first chapter, disability is perceived as a result of interaction between biological, psychological and social factors (Gottlieb et al. 2010).

The biopsychosocial model has evolved. It was preceded by the International Classification of Impairments, Disabilities and Handicaps (ICIDH), published by the WHO (1980), which was the first conceptualization taking into account the wide range of personal, social and environmental disability experiences affecting the three stages of physical and social integration. In the ICIDH approach, inclusion criteria include three elements: impairments, disabilities and handicaps. Disability is a limitation or lack of ability to perform activities in a manner or within a range considered normal for a human being. Such restrictions are caused by impairments, which are losses or abnormalities in the structure or function of the psychological, physiological or anatomical organism. Handicaps, in turn, are caused by impairments and disabilities, which limit or make it impossible to fulfil a role recognized as normal depending on age, gender and social and cultural factors (Fig. 1).

Fig. 1 The phenomenon of disability in the conceptualization of ICIDH (*Source* Based on World Health Organization 1980)

Further work on understanding the nature of disability, the relationship between personal, social and environmental factors has led to the replacement of ICIDH with the International Classification of Functioning, Disability and Health (ICF). In the ICF approach, interactions between health components include (WHO 2001):

1. health conditions (defined as disorders or diseases), body structures (defined as anatomical parts of the body), body functions (defined as the physiological functions of body systems);
2. an activity is defined as the execution of a task or action by an individual;
3. participation is defined as involvement in a life situation;
4. environmental factors comprise the physical, social and attitudinal environments in which people live and conduct their lives;
5. personal factors include gender, race, age, fitness, lifestyle, habits, upbringing, coping styles, social background, education, profession and a variety of other possible characteristics of individuals.

The functioning of a person at the level of the body and therefore the ability to perform tasks (activities) and/or participate in life situations are understood as functions of complex relations between the state of health and personal and environmental factors (Fig. 2).

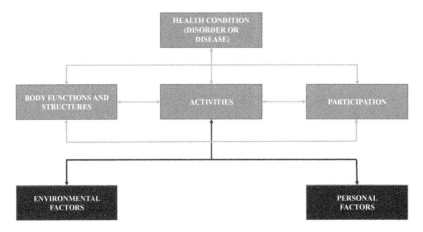

Fig. 2 Interactions between the components of the ICF (*Source* Based on World Health Organization 2001)

ICIDH and ICF conceptualizations contain a contemporary understanding of the nature of impairments and disability, indicating the limitations that are imposed on individuals by their own bodies, and on handicaps that are additional factors imposed on people with disabilities by their environments, cultures and institutions. Further research into the use of ICF (as a tool for statistics, clinical practice, social policy and education) has led to the modifications mentioned above. The development of ICF was based, inter alia, on opinions from representatives of organisations dealing with disability. The risk of medicalization, dehumanization and increased classification of people associated with the use of ICF was pointed out, which raised concern among scientists and other professionals dealing with disability. Therefore, the need for active cooperation with organisations of disabled persons was emphasized (Priestley et al. 2010; Lundälv et al. 2015). The concept of handicap was removed from the classification because it focused only on the physical dimension of disability, and therefore, participation restriction was introduced. The concept of disability that has been fully adopted by the ICF is a concept *with a bio-psychosocial dimension* (Hurst 2003 after Lundälv et al. 2015). It recognizes socio-environmental factors, socio-demographic factors and behavioural factors that dictate the subjective experience of living with disabilities (Jette 2006). As pointed out by Robert L. Metts (2008), this understanding is important from a political point of view, since it leads inevitably to the conclusion that policies and strategies aimed at increasing the social and economic access of people with disabilities must go beyond traditional medical and rehabilitative approaches to disability. Increasing the functional capacity of people with disabilities must take into account a wide spectrum of problems related to the prevention, removal or alleviation of a wide range of additional environmental, cultural and institutional barriers (Metts 2008, pp. 22–23). The biopsychosocial model evolves and benefits from the constant development of medical and social models. As emphasized by Gottlieb, Myhill and Blanck, it is a new model and its contribution to the employment opportunities of people with disabilities is still unclear. However, it can be assumed that by focusing on social and environmental factors, like the social model, it will have a positive impact on the employment opportunities of people with disabilities (Gottlieb et al. 2010).

1.2 Exclusion from the Labour Market and New Perspectives

Dissemination of the assumptions of social model, and then the biopsychosocial models, revealed the real nature of disability and contributed to a change in the approach to work and employment of disabled people in the countries of Western civilization. These models have become important tools in defining the phenomenon of disability, playing an important role in defining the strategies that governments and societies and international structures are developing to help meet the needs of people with disabilities. The increase in employment of disabled people, as shown in the previous chapter, is still unsatisfactory, in most economically developed countries. Determinants of the increase in the employment level of disabled people are the result of a complex impact of many factors acting on the principle of synergy.

In the countries of the former Eastern bloc, the long-term policy of excluding disabled persons from the labour market or directing them to the protected labour market in closed workplaces is firmly fixed in social practices and attitudes of people. An example is Poland, in which the practices prevalent in the previous system (the real socialism economy) dominate the practice of employers, social workers and job agents, resulting in the treatment of people with disabilities in an objective and paternalistic way. Which leads the researchers to ask whether in the present system of market economy people with disabilities exist for the institutions or whether institutions exist for people? Analyses of the functioning of professional activation and employment practices of disabled people point to the latter direction (Giermanowska and Racław 2016).

However, also a liberal economy based on profit, in which financial crises occur, does not create good prospects for employment of disabled people. In the labour markets with high unemployment, people with disabilities compete for jobs prepared exclusively for people with disabilities. Guy Standing (2014b) points to the relationship between the disabled and the precariat. Increasing bills for social benefits for people with disabilities have prompted governments of many countries at the beginning of the twenty-first century to reduce them by applying a more rigorous verification of medical disability. It was also a way to increase the "employability" of people with disabilities. A more rigorous verification of disabled people's ability to work combined with limited access to social benefits has become a practice in many countries. The procedures used to separate the real from the "pretend" disabled have caused people with disabilities many humiliations, the need to undergo more thorough, intimidating and stigmatizing tests (Standing 2014a). However, disabled people with limited life choices are more likely to fall into the precariat category than they will receive stable, dignified employment conditions.

They fall victim to the global flexible labour market, the precarious cycle of inconvenience and uncertainty (Standing 2014b).

Considering these structural conditions, the British sociologist Colin Barnes (2012) claims that solving the problem of employment for disabled people requires a new configuration of disability and work concepts. A new configuration of work could be based on recognizing as work everyday tasks that people do. In the case of disabled people, these would be everyday tasks related to disability. Here, he refers to the studies of Corbin and Strauss (1988), who identified three types of work related to "illness management". These are: (a) "illness work", including activities such as organisation and administration of medicines, physiotherapy, etc.; (b) "everyday work", i.e. home activities and interactions with family and professionals; (c) "biographical work"—strategies that people with disabilities employ to give value to their everyday life, they may include the development of various adaptation skills and explaining their state to others (Corbin and Strauss 1988).

According to Barnes, the growing involvement of people with disabilities in the development and delivery of services related to disability should be understood as work. People with disabilities can appear in many roles—as producers of services provided to disabled people and as consumers a wide range of services. The introduction of various self-service systems in the area of services provided means, for example, that people with disabilities become employers for many professionals supporting them. They are responsible for the recruitment and financing of services, and here, their knowledge and skills are similar to running a "small business". These new solutions make the support and benefits system less stigmatizing, and people with disabilities as producers and service consumers gain respect in the orthodox work environment (Barnes 2012).

At this point, it is also worth referring to the publications of other sociologists who, in considering the growing unemployment and inability to provide employment for all, postulate an appreciation of various types of non-profit work and their new cultural anchoring. One such proposal is the concept of civil society of the German sociologist Ulrich Beck (2000), which presents it as an alternative to the work society.

The new model of society is based on both paid work and civic work. Civil society is created by citizens involved in various types of work, including in paid and full-time work (according to ability and needs), and civil work, which includes voluntary work, for example, in art, culture, politics and parental care for children and their upbringing (Beck 2000). The new division of labour in the multi-active society goes well beyond the distribution of paid work, in guaranteeing certain entitlements till now linked to employment (e.g. retirement pensions, health care) also to people performing different types of work. Including civic work in the field of social policy, as Beck emphasizes, is a method of counteracting unemployment and the implementation of civil rights (Beck 2000).

The American sociologist Richard Sennett (2006), in his analysis of the disintegration of industrial capitalism and the birth of a new, global and flexible economy, proposes a new cultural anchoring of the sphere of human work. The new work ethic should be based on three basic values: narrative continuity, usefulness and the ideal of craftsmanship. The achievement of narrative continuity is possible due to the introduction of various parallel institutional solutions that give people a sense of security and anchorage in the event of job loss (e.g. through temporary employment agencies run by trade unions for their members, work sharing, guaranteed income). Usefulness is linked raising status of people performing various types of unpaid work, but important for society and being a public good (such as volunteering, care for children and the elderly). The ideal of craftsmanship is related to masterful accomplishment of tasks, and not loyalty towards institutions (Sennett 2006).

The problem of changes in work and employment models is connected with the choice of lifestyle policy. Referring to the life policy perspective adopted by Giddens (1991), disabled people in the era of late modernity should have the opportunity to choose different lifestyles, based not only on performing paid work, but also on engaging in other activities that are useful to the society (Giermanowska and Racław 2014). However, this is connected, which results from the above-quoted considerations, the change in cultural values and the reconstruction of the model of the welfare state.

Reconfiguration of the concept of work could be not simply an alternative but a complement to activities increasing the participation of disabled people in the labour market, but it requires changes in the cultural values that underlie inequalities in the labour market (Barnes and Roulstone 2005, p. 324). The reforms of the welfare state should be thorough and change the existing ideas about the role of the social benefits system. Giddens, referring to the policy of life, emphasizes that "the social benefits system is not just about avoiding risk. Increasingly, it is also related to positive changes in lifestyle" (Giddens 2007). Creation of conditions for the implementation of a chosen lifestyle implements a model based on civil rights, in which "a disabled person is more than just someone who can participate in the life of a wider community [through emancipation], it is a person who 'can and has the right to do so' As a full-fledged citizen, and what's more, he also has the right to articulate his needs just like any other (non-disabled) member of society" (Mikołajczyk-Lerman 2013, p. 36). The citizen also has the right to "one's own" policy of life. However, the ineffectiveness of the tools offered to implement personal choices—in the promotion of a rights-based model—will lead to new social problems. This phenomenon was described by Giermanowska and Racław, in their analysis of the professional lives of disabled university graduates. The change of political system in Poland (1989) created for disabled people unprecedented (in the economy of real socialism) educational opportunities, including at the level of higher education. However, this was not accompanied by easier access to the labour market. As a result, there was an increase in the number of unemployed—university graduates who were certified disabled (Giermanowska and Racław 2014).

In the second half of the twentieth century, the practices of employing people with disabilities began to change. The spread of the social and biopsychosocial models of disability have done a lot for changing the approach to the phenomenon of disability and professional roles of disabled people. The practice of the "normalization" policy to help people with disabilities achieve decent living conditions and valuable social roles has an impact (Oliver 1990; Barnes and Mercer 2003). However, we point to its limitations.

2 THE RESULTS OF THE RESEARCH IDENTIFYING FACTORS OF ACTIVITY OF PEOPLE WITH DISABILITIES ON THE LABOUR MARKET

Modern researchers emphasize the importance of many different factors for the employment of disabled people on the demand and supply side of the labour market. They also point to the need to take into account the impact of procedures and practices used by social services to enable people with disabilities to work, to remain in employment or return to the labour market. The impact of these categories of factors is noted—in varying degrees—in most countries—regardless of the disability policy model in use. Some factors or their bundles create barriers in accessing the labour market and are referred to as demotivators of professional activity of disabled people. As a result, "The main picture of lower participation in paid work for the disabled is consistent across studies (Kittelsaa, Wik, and Tøssebro 2015) and across countries (Bliksvær and Hanssen 2006; Holland et al. 2011; Lillestø and Sandvin 2014; Sainsbury and Coleman-Fountain 2013; Zaidi 2011)" (Bliksvær 2018, p. 7).

In many countries, therefore, research is conducted, which records the barriers to professional activity of people with disabilities. These barriers can be identified at the following levels:

- macro (the level of organisation of society as a whole and its main social institutions, i.e. culture, law, economy),
- meso (the level of local communities and local social institutions),
- micro (that is at the level of the individual, including his family situation, socio-demographic characteristics, personality and motivation).

With regard to the maintenance of persons with disabilities in the labour resources, Swedish researchers (Östlund and Johansson 2018) identified 4 groups of factors that determine work active people with disability. They explored how people with disabilities perceive their inclusion in working life. The sample comprises a group of working people experiencing different kinds of physical and sensory disabilities. Östlund and Johansson (2018) described barriers such as:

a. the environmental participation barrier which encompasses social, communicative and physical hinder to take part on equal terms;
b. the jungle of devices;
c. the catch-22 situations which relates to conflicting rules and goals of welfare agencies;
d. the inflexibility of welfare services—which refers to the inflexibility and lack of coordination of health care, rehabilitation-, home- and transport services with being a worker and having scheduled shifts at daytime.

The first group of factors means barriers that interfere with the entry and job maintenance of people with disabilities in the workplace, such as architectural unavailability, high noise in the workplace interfering with people with hearing problems, maladjustment of workplaces and the environment. They have the nature of communication and physical limitations in the workplace, for which an employer may be responsible in accordance with national law (this is the case in Sweden). These barriers can also occur outside the workplace in the public sphere, affecting the professional activity of disabled people, e.g. increasing their fatigue and reducing work efficiency.

The jungle of devices means the uncertainty of people with disabilities in a situation of change. This uncertainty results from lack of knowledge who to turn to, when technical support or workplace adaptation is required. In Sweden, the scale and level of support in technical devices and the coordination of services are locally diverse. This results in a sense of fragmentation of support and over-complication in the process of receiving help (similar allegations are directed at the Polish support system for people with disabilities [Rudnicki 2014]).

The catch-22 situations describe the lack of coordination in terms of goals and actions between key institutional actors responsible for keeping people with disabilities in labour resources. In Sweden, these are the social insurance offices and employment agencies. Discrepancies in activities are evident in determining how to deal with the specific health situation of a disabled person: whether to keep them on the labour market or deactivate them. "Laws aiming to protect the right of people with disabilities to employment and equal participation will be ineffective if they are not coordinated and if collaborations between stakeholders do not function. Furthermore, welfare authorities have to improve their understanding of how to create anti-discriminatory practices, instead of individualising discrimination by viewing it as connected to the individual's identity rather than unjust aspects of the welfare system" (Östlund and Johansson 2018, p. 23).

The inflexibility of welfare services is associated with restrictions on access to services due to their strictly defined time or place of delivery, which interferes with the hours of work of a disabled person. The flexibility of rehabilitation and healthcare services is particularly important. Rigid working hours of services for people with disabilities cause absence of those rehabilitated at the place of work.

The barriers described by Swedish researchers encountered by working disabled people show synergetic impact of factors coming from two levels of social organisation (macro and meso): from the legal and economic system and from the local environment (employers and representatives of social services, characteristics of the local environment). The existence of limitations in taking up and continuing employment by disabled people results from the interdependent connection of barriers generated from different levels of organisation of social life. The maladjustment of the workplace itself may not be a sufficient "repulsive factor", but in connection with the lack of flexible hours of health services and a sense of uncertainty caused by a lack of information about support at the local level, it may contribute to abandoning work or abandoning employment.

The importance of the meso-level is also emphasized by researchers describing and analysing the relationships between employing organisations, work and care (Bowlby et al. 2010). "The employing organization is a purposive entity in which policies and practices operate, and employers and employees can both 'care about' and 'care for' others. (...) we can envisage employing organizations trying to realise particular aims and goals relating to 'caring' for their employees by actively selecting their paths through a map or a terrain that includes legislation, an economic context, company finances and goals, and the needs of employees as these shift with demographic trends" (Bowlby et al. 2010, pp. 142–143). The employing organisations create their own "care policies" that is the practices and procedures of care in the workplace. Organisational cultures are de facto cultures of care and change with the internal and external environment of the organisation. An individual employee, when planning his routes, will adapt it to the actions of employers and personal events (such as childbirth, worse health, the need to undertake rehabilitation). Workplaces can be a part of a care network. Care inside work also means informal support practices that are provided by a group of colleagues or a supervisor. The perspective of the analysis of the care inside work is particularly important and fruitful in research on the employment of people with disabilities.

Research on the meso- and micro-level often focuses on the barriers perceived by employers in the area of employment and retention of persons with disability. Sharma et al. (2018) reviewed international literature in the discussed area. On this basis, they identified the common points of concern of employers about employing individuals with disabilities. These are:

a. job-related performance dilemma,
b. lack of professional skills,
c. training and development issues,
d. attitudes of co-workers,
e. workplace modifications/accessibility/accommodations,
f. understanding of the concept of disability,
g. legal obligations,
h. pre-requisite emphasis on aesthetic and self-presentation skills, important in some industries, e.g. hotel industry.

Polish research experience confirms the universality of the indicated concerns (Giermanowska 2014b, p. 63). In them, problems identified by employers that limit the employment of disabled people in a post-transformation country have been identified:

a. administrative: related to bureaucratic support for subsidies granted by government institutions and unstable legal regulations,
b. social: prejudices and stereotypes identified in both employers and other employees,
c. financial: that is higher labour costs (resulting from lower labour productivity, special entitlements of people with disabilities),
d. organisational: related to the adaptation of workplaces and the type of work to the capabilities of disabled people and the need to distribute tasks to other colleagues,
e. qualifications: resulting from low or inadequate qualifications of disabled persons and their passive attitudes towards finding a job,
f. information: that is the lack of knowledge of employers about the possibilities and ways of acquiring disabled employees or using their professional potential,
g. infrastructure: it is created by unadapted local infrastructure, which should support employees (communication, rehabilitation and health services),
h. local support: institutional and social environment poorly supporting local entrepreneurs who want to employ people with disabilities.

In addition, Polish research has demonstrated the importance of cultural and social factors in motivating employers to employ disabled people. Giermanowska and Racław (2014, p. 123) emphasize that the achievement of higher professional activity of disabled people requires not only improvement of economic instruments, legal instruments, development of services or multi-sectoral cooperation, but also cultural changes shaping the attitudes of employers towards such employees. These theses were confirmed by the results of research into the conditions of adaptation of workplaces for people with disabilities in Polish enterprises (Czarzasty et al. 2017). They showed that Polish employers lack general knowledge about disability, which results in avoiding the employment of people with functional deficits. In addition, some small companies treated fees for "not recruiting" people with disabilities (appearing in the quota model) as a tax obligation and not an alternative to employment for people with disabilities (Czarzasty et al. 2017, p. 32).

There are also reports of researchers focusing on the individual perspective and the individual determinants of taking up professional activity or returning to the labour market in a situation of functional deficits or becoming disabled. Among the factors that identify the barriers on the side of the individual are those resulting from the attitudes and characteristics of disabled people (Struck-Peregończyk 2015, p. 58). These include: age-related restrictions, contraindications for health reasons, lack of motivation to work, lack of earning needs, income conflict (work-pension), low self-esteem, need for constant medical care, lack of or low professional training, lack of knowledge about ways of looking for a job and activity of support institutions, higher morbidity, subjective sense of poor health, lower mobility and efficiency of disabled people, lower quality of work and excessive pay expectations.

Hungarian researchers (Kertész et al. 2017) indicated three key factors conditioning the motivation for people with disabilities to work in their country. The data gathered during the interviews supported by a preliminarily prepared questionnaire recorded by social affairs specialists of the National Office for Rehabilitation and Social Affairs can be taken as coming from a quasi-representative national sample (Kertész et al. 2017, p. 109) The analyses of data obtained among people of working age indicated that the following are key is disabled people taking up employment:

a. possessed skills that were related to the level of education (a higher level of education gave better opportunities on the local labour market, but also shaped the attitude of openness to the world in building social relations, which could result in getting a job),
b. the number of years of inactivation, including those related to unemployment: a longer stay outside the labour market causes a decrease in motivation and the emergence of the attitude of learned helplessness,
c. the social and economic situation of the family, especially the economic situation; The support received from the family can have a motivating effect on returning to the labour market. At the same time, family background turned out to be a significant but hidden factor in the study, which, once included in the analysis, enabled better interpretation of the data.

In the case of one of the identified variables—education—there are polemical reports. In general, there is a consensus that a higher level of education contributes to reducing social inequalities by enabling people with disabilities to find employment on the open labour market. Trond Bliksvær (2018), however, draws attention to the need for caution in the interpretation of the impact of the level of education in obtaining and retaining work by disabled persons.

The researcher argues that "In research there is substantial support for the idea that the effect of education is greater for disabled people than for non-disabled people, but the magnitude of the effect varies substantially between studies, in part due to different methodological procedures and possibilities in the data. Furthermore, the substantial differences in employment rates between the two groups also affect our observations about the effect of educational level on employment" (Bliksvær 2018, p. 8). His analyses conducted on Norwegian data indicate that the relationship between education and employment is not as unambiguous as it is commonly accepted, and one should employ caution when formulating recommendations "that higher education is the main route to reduced inequalities and greater societal inclusion for disabled people" (Bliksvær 2018, p. 16). These observations are also confirmed by the results of Polish research conducted among disabled students and graduates of higher education institutions, for whom gaining a higher education did not mean receiving a job consistent with qualifications and sometimes they did not enter the labour market at all. The research results showed that the majority of graduates functioned on the temporary labour market or performed work not conducive to the development of their careers. Barriers in entering the labour market and creating a satisfactory career path caused an increase in frustration among young people with disabilities, creating social problems (Giermanowska et al. 2015; Giermanowska and Racław 2014).

In turn, the factor related to the family situation should be understood in a broader context. Kertész et al. (2017) indicate the importance of the professional status of family members, both as an indirect and direct factor, modifying the level of motivation to work of disabled persons. The indirect influence of the family background is related to the family socialization process. Hungarian researchers concluded that the presence in the family of people in paid employment creates a pattern of acceptable behaviour resulting from internalized values (work as an important value in the family environment). On the other hand, the presence of people in paid employment reduces the motivation to work of people with disabilities in a direct manner. Probably this is connected with the lack of necessity of obtaining additional income (as the social security benefit is sufficient).

The meaning of family background in the context of socialization to work and shaping in children the readiness to taking up challenges in the future is confirmed by other researchers. Some research results suggest that one of the reasons for not looking for a job by young people with disabilities is the negative attitude of the family (Struck-Pergonczyk 2017, p. 105). The negative impact of the family on professional activation is linked with parental over-protectiveness and convincing the young person that work has a negative impact on their health. The family also suggests that such a person will not be able to cope on the labour market, especially the open one. Families might also discourage the young person with a disability from working because of the fear of losing benefits that are a stable source of income of the young people and their families.

The family situation of people with disabilities is a multidimensional factor influencing their motivation to take up paid work. The presence in the family of people earning money, the economic situation of the family, and having children dependent on disabled people are all of importance. Being a parent with disability introduces additional determinants of professional activity. Polish research has shown that undertaking work is considered in the context of anticipated difficulties in combining work and private life (Dziekan et al. 2018). Polish parents with disabilities pointed to the importance of both formal accommodations and workplace support (flexible working time, remote work), public services (mainly transport to the workplace), as well as the importance of informal factors related to the openness of employers to the question of combining professional and family life, and work culture focused on the employee, including on care inside work (e.g. current response to the problems of the employee and his family, the ability to modify the tasks in agreement with colleagues, convenient working hours). Good relations with superiors and colleagues have often been a variable of time and professional position—the longer a parent worked in a given organisation and occupied a higher professional position, the more often he had greater opportunities to negotiate working conditions and modify them in an informal way.

Nevertheless, Kertész et al. (2017, p. 115) state that the results obtained by the Hungarian team (regarding the importance of skills and education, the period of inactivation and the socio-economic situation of the family) coincide with the results of research conducted in other countries in the area of vocational rehabilitation. In general, research in this area distinguishes three sets of obstacles related to the return of workers with disabilities to the labour market. The following are important:

a. personal characteristic: age, gender, family and social background, education, training and skills, work history and experience, physical or mental condition, impairment and functional limits;
b. psychological factors: personal experience of illness and disability, perceptions and expectations, attitudes, beliefs, emotions, mood, coping strategies, motivation, effort, incentives and uncertainty;
c. social factors: culture, surrounding health, sickness, disability and work, labour market forces, social and occupational barriers, discrimination, social exclusion and financial (dis)incentive.

Similar results were obtained at the turn of the twentieth and twenty-first centuries by American researchers who established important determinants of return to work that may have long-term effects (Baldwin and Johnson 2001, pp. 16–17):

Demographic Characteristics

1. *Gender*: men are more likely to return to work than women.
2. *Age*: the probability of return to work decreases with age.
3. *Race*: African-Americans are less likely to return to work than white-Americans.
4. *Marital status*: married men (unmarried women) are more likely to return to work than unmarried men (married women).

Human Capital Characteristics

1. *Education*: the probability of return to work increases with education.
2. *Experience*: the probability of return to work increases with work experience prior to injury.

Economic Incentives

1. *Wages*: the higher the expected wage, the higher the probability of return to work.
2. *Replacement rate*: the probability of return to work decreases as the ratio of indemnity benefits to pre-injury. Estimates of the benefit elasticity, however, are inconsistent across studies.

Marjorie J. Baldwin and William G. Johnson (2001, p. 24) also drew attention to the necessity to adjust disability policy measures, including activation on the labour market according to the phase of life in which the disability arose. American researchers stressed that people who acquired disability in childhood or disabled from birth will seek to enforce their rights of equal access to good-quality education and labour market institutions. Persons who have become disabled as adults will, on the other hand, enforce the right to return to work, vocational rehabilitation, provision of adequate work places and benefits in the period of absence related to sickness or disability.

Finally, while analysing the individual, we need to emphasize the influence of psychological variables, i.e. experiencing one's own disability and illness and satisfaction with life, as modifiers of motivation to look for a job for disabled people and their professional activity. Research by psychologist Dorota Wierzbicka-Wiszejko (2008, p. 60) conducted among people with disabilities in Poland indicates that there is a strong relationship between the acceptance of one's disability and professional activity. Satisfaction with life results from self-acceptance and professional work can strengthen this satisfaction. The author emphasizes that professional work plays a significant role in shaping a positive image of oneself, but this does not take place if work does not correspond to the aspirations and qualifications of people with disabilities. This explains the increase in frustration observed by researchers in young and educated people with disabilities (greater than their able-bodied colleagues) who cannot find employment that suits their aspirations and professional qualifications (see Burchardt 2005).

3 "Bundle of Factors" Model

A review of the literature on the subject and research reports related to broad conditions and particular factors affecting the professional activity of disabled people, allowed us to develop our own "bundle of factors" model. We present it in Fig. 3.

According to the analysis carried out in the previous section, we distinguish three levels of social organisation that affect the professional activity of disabled people. The presented scheme is illustrated by three circles:

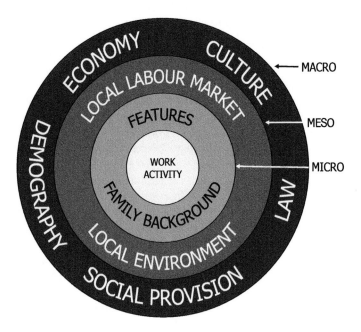

Fig. 3 "Bundle of factors" model (*Source* Own analysis)

macro, meso, micro. We accept that these levels interact with each other. We reject structural determinism in which the macro-level determines the behaviour of the individual. At the same time, we are not advocates of methodological individualism. In our approach, the professional activity of disabled people is determined by multiple levels and factors. Factors belonging to different levels influence each other, giving various effects. Some of them rely on mutual reinforcement (in a specific historical and cultural context), others neutralize each other (also in a specific context). They lead to emergent effects, i.e. new phenomena that are the result of interaction between elements of the structure (see Boudon 1993). In Table 1, we have listed selected factors that can be identified at individual levels of the social organisation, affecting the professional activity of disabled people.

Table 1 Selected factors from various levels of social organisation affecting the activity of people with disabilities

	Macro-level
Culture	Social values that build social order (e.g. egalitarianism, justice, solidarity, trust).
	Social codes of respect for individuals (e.g. the imperative "take care of yourself", "be independent").
	Social norms concerning the role of the disabled and the sick in society.
	Cultural stereotypes relating to specific social groups and phenomena.
	Work ethic and care ethics.
Demographic development	Population resources: population, population structure by age, sex and marital status.
	The course of population processes: fertility, morbidity and mortality, migrations, population ageing and urbanization.
	Reproduction of the condition and structure of the population.
Economy	The level of the country's economic development affecting:
	• generosity of social benefits,
	• number of jobs,
	• level of pay,
	• development of technical infrastructure,
	• technological advance.
Law	National anti-discrimination law.
	Segregation regulations (addressed to people with disabilities as a special category).
	Labour law regulations.
	Implementation of international regulations in national law (ILO, UN, COE, EU).

(continued)

Table 1 (continued)

Social provision	Social benefits due to temporary and long-term incapacity to work.
	Public social services in the field of:
	• professional and social rehabilitation,
	• health care,
	• social assistance and help (addressed to people with disabilities and their families),
	• professional activation and career counselling.
	Educational services (from school education to lifelong learning).
	Public transport services.
	Preparation and professionalism of social services.
	Information and educational tools related to the introduction of disabled people into the labour market (addressed to people with disabilities and employers).
	• Subsidizing jobs.
	Meso-level
Local environment	Features of the local environment: level of urbanization, level of socio-economic development, development of social and technical infrastructure, demographic development and adaptation of public space (universal design).
	Features of the local community: empathy, support and acceptance for the presence of disabled people in the public space.
Local labour market	The condition and structure of local labour resources.
	Availability of suitable vacancies on the local labour market.
	The level of remuneration on the local labour market.
	Occurrence and diffusion of good practices of employing disabled people.
	Knowledge of local employers regarding disability.
	Knowledge of local employers regarding the possibility of receiving support from public funds and public services in the field of employment and retention of a disabled person at work.
	Openness of local employers to employing and retaining disabled people (organisational culture—care inside work, diversity management, CSR).

(continued)

Table 1 (continued)

	Micro-level
Family background	Features of the family environment: a. family of origin: overprotection of the family, encouraging/discouraging attitude towards challenges and independence, family system of values and norms, dominant socialization message and economic situation of the family; b. own family: having children—their number, age, having an earning spouse/partner.
Features	Socio-demographic characteristics of an individual: age, sex, degree, type and permanence of disability, phase of life, when disabilities arose, marital and family status, level of education, professional experience and skills. Experiencing health and disability: stability or dynamics of changes in health and disability, acceptance of one's disability. Other psychological factors: general satisfaction with life, motivation to act, including professional work, self-esteem. Economic situation: having income and having social benefits (stability and amount of social benefits).

Source Own analysis

The list of selected factors determining the employment of disabled people presented in Table 1 is certainly not exhaustive. However, we have collected those that are repeated in research conducted over the last two decades in various European countries and in the USA. They point to the need to include in the public policy on disability and HR policies of specific organisations of many variables that will determine the success of employment of disabled people. This corresponds to the idea of a multidimensional and inter-sectional view of the phenomenon of disability, which is postulated by researchers associated with the orientation of Disability Studies. Many of these factors are of a sociocultural nature, which means that economic incentives and legal recommendations will not be sufficient to change the professional activity rate of people with disabilities in the short- and long-term perspective.

REFERENCES

Assistive Technologies for People with Disabilities. 2018. Brussels, European Union. Accessed July 9, 2019. http://www.europarl.europa.eu/stoa/en/document/EPRS_IDA(2018)603218.

Baldwin, Marjorie J., and William G. Johnson. 2001. "Dispelling the Myths About Work Disability." Prepared for the 1998 IRRA Research Volume *New Approaches to Disability in the Workplace*.
Barnes, Colin. 2012. "Re-thinking Disability, Work and Welfare." *Sociology Compass* 6 (6): 472–484.
Barnes, Colin, and Alan Roulstone. 2005. "'Work' Is a Four-Letter Word: Disability, Work and Welfare." In *Working Futures? Disabled People, Policy and Social Inclusion*, edited by Alan Roulstone and Colin Barnes, 315–327. Bristol: The Policy Press University of Bristol.
Barnes, Colin, and Geof Mercer. 2003. *Disability*. Cambridge: Polity Press.
Beck, Ulrich. 2000. *The Brave New World of Work*. Cambridge: Polity Press.
Berger, Ronald J. 2013. *Introducing Disability Studies*. Boulder: Lynne Rienner Publishers.
Blanck, Peter. 2008. "The Right to Live in the World: Disability Yesterday, Today and Tomorrow." *Texas Journal on Civil Liberties and Civil Rights* 13: 367–401.
Bliksvær, Trond. 2018. "Disability, Labour Market Participation and the Effect of Educational Level: Compared to What?" *Scandinavian Journal of Disability Research* 20 (1): 6–17. https://doi.org/10.16993/sjdr.3.
Boudon, Raymond. 1993. *Effets pervers et ordre social*. Paris: Presses Universitaires de France.
Bowlby, Sophia, Linda McKie, Susan Gregory, and Isobel MacPherson. 2010. *Interdependency and Care Over the Life Course*. London and New York: Routledge.
Burchardt, Tania. 2005. *The Education and Employment of Disabled Young People: Frustrated Ambition*. Bristol: The Polity Press for Joseph Rowntree Foundation.
Castells. Manuel. 1996. *The Rise of the Network Society*. Oxford: Blackwell.
Corbin, Juliet, and Anselm L. Strauss. 1988. *Unending Work and Care: Managing Chronic Illness at Home*. San Francisco: Jossey-Bass Publishers.
Czarzasty, Jan, Małgorzata Koziarek, and Dominik Owczarek. 2017. *Adaptacja miejsca pracy dla starszych i niepełnosprawnych pracowników w Polsce* [Workplace Adaptation to Older and Disabled Workers in Poland]. Warszawa: ISP.
Dziekan, Jacek, Mateusz Pawłowicz, and Agnieszka Smoder. 2018. "Zabezpieczenie społeczne i aktywność zawodowa rodziców z niepełnosprawnościami." In *"Byliśmy jak z kosmosu". Między (nie)wydolnością środowiska a potrzebami rodziców z niepełnosprawnościami*, edited by Dorota Wiszejko-Wierzbicka, Mariola Racław, and Agnieszka Wołowicz-Ruszkowska, 95–114. Warszawa: Instytut Spraw Publicznych.
Finkelstein, Vic. 1980. *Attitudes and Disabled People*. New York: World Rehabilitation Fund.

Foley, Alan, and Beth A. Ferri. 2012. "Technology for People, Not Disabilities: Ensuring Access and Inclusion." *Journal of Research in Special Educational Needs* 12 (4): 192–200.

Garbat, Marcin. 2012. *Zatrudnianie i rehabilitacja zawodowa osób z niepełnosprawnością w Europie*. Zielona Góra: Oficyna Wydawnicza Uniwersytetu Zielonogórskiego.

Giddens, Anthony. 1991. *Modernity and Self-Identity: Self and Society in the Late Modern Age*. Stanford: Stanford University Press.

Giddens, Anthony. 2007. *Europe in the Global Age*. Cambridge: Polity Press.

Giermanowska, Ewa, ed. 2014a. *Zatrudniając niepełnosprawnych. Dobre praktyki w Polsce i innych krajach Europy*. Kraków: Akademia Górniczo-Hutnicza im. S. Staszica w Krakowie.

Giermanowska, Ewa 2014b. „Zatrudnianie niepełnosprawnych pracowników. Oczekiwania pracodawców." In *Zatrudniając niepełnosprawnych. Dobre praktyki w Polsce i innych krajach Europy*, edited by Ewa Giermanowska, 61–114. Kraków: Akademia Górniczo-Hutnicza im. S. Staszica w Krakowie.

Giermanowska, Ewa, and Mariola Racław. 2014. „Pomiędzy polityką życia, emancypacją i jej pozorowaniem. Pytania o nowy model polityki społecznej wobec zatrudniania osób niepełnosprawnych" [Between Politics of Life, Emancipation and Appearances: Questions Regarding a New Model of Social Policy of Disabled Persons Employment]. *Studia Socjologiczne* 2 (213): 107–127.

Giermanowska, Ewa, Agnieszka Kumaniecka-Wiśniewska, and Elżbieta Zakrzewska-Manterys. 2015. *Niedokończona emancypacja: wejście niepełnosprawnych absolwentów szkół wyższych na rynek pracy*. Warszawa: Wydawnictwa Uniwersytetu Warszawskiego.

Giermanowska, Ewa, and Mariola Racław. 2016. "Commercialisation of Occupational Development Services: People for the Institutions or Institutions for the People." *Studia Humanistyczne AGH* 15 (4): 21–33.

Gottlieb, Aaron, William N. Myhil, and Peter Blanck. 2010. "Employment of People with Disabilities." In *International Encyclopedia of Rehabilitation*. New York: Center for International Rehabilitation Research Information and Exchange (CIRRIE).

Hurst, Rachel. 2003. "The International Disability Rights Movement and the ICF." *Disability and Rehabilitation* 25: 572–576.

Jette, Alan M. 2006. "Toward a Common Language for Function, Disability, and Health." *Physical Therapy* 86 (5): 726–734.

Kertész, Andrienn, Beatrix Séllei, and Lajos Izsó. 2017. "Key Factors of Disabled People's Working Motivation: An Empirical Study Based on a Hungarian Sample." *Periodica Polytechnica Social and Management Sciences* 25 (2): 108–116. https://doi.org/10.3311/PPso.10459.

Lundälv, Jörgen, Marie Törnbom, Per-Olof Larsson, and Katharina S. Sunnerhagen. 2015. "Awareness and the Arguments for and Against the International Classification of Functioning, Disability and Health Among Representatives of Disability Organisations." *International Journal of Environmental Research and Public Health* 12: 3293–3300.
Lunt, Neil, and Patricia Thornton. 1994. "Disability and Employment: Towards an Understanding of Discourse and Policy." *Disability & Society* 9 (2): 223–238. Published online: 23 February 2007.
Metts, Robert L. 2008. "Rethinking Disability and Corporate Responsibility." *Journal of Leadership, Accountability, and Ethics* (Fall): 19–27. http://www.na-businesspress.com/jlae/template_fall08.pdf.
Mikołajczyk-Lerman, Grażyna. 2013. *Między wykluczeniem a integracją – realizacja praw dziecka niepełnosprawnego i jego rodziny. Analiza socjologiczna.* Łódź: Wydawnictwo Uniwersytetu Łódzkiego.
Myhill, William N., and Peter Blanck. 2009. "Disability and Aging: Historical and Contemporary Challenges." *Marquette Elder's Advisor* 11 (1): 47–80 (Article 4).
Oliver, Mike. 1990. *The Politics of Disablement.* London: Palgrave.
Östlund, Gunnel, and Gun Johansson. 2018. "Remaining in Workforce—Employment Barriers for People with Disabilities in a Swedish Context." *Scandinavian Journal of Disability Research* 20 (1): 18–25. https://doi.org/10.16993/sjdr.4.
Priestley, Mark, Lisa Waddington, and Carlotta Bessozi. 2010. "Towards an Agenda for Disability Research in Europe: Learning from Disabled People's Organisations." *Disability & Society* 25: 731–746.
Rudnicki, Seweryn. 2014. "Niepełnosprawność i złożoność." *Studia Socjologiczne* 2 (213): 43–61.
Sennett, Richard. 2006. *The Culture of New Capitalism.* New Haven and London: Yale University Press.
Shapiro, Joseph P. 1994. *No Pity: People with Disabilities Forging a New Civil Rights Movement.* New York: Times Books.
Sharma, Ambuj, Martin Zsarnoczky, and Anna Dunay. 2018. "An Empirical Study on the Influences of Management's Attitudes Toward Employees with Disabilities in the Hospitality Sector." *Polish Journal of Management Studies* 18 (2): 331–343.
Standing, Guy. 2014a. *The Precariat Charter: From Denizens to Citizens.* London: Bloomsbury.
Standing, Guy. 2014b. *The Precariat: The New Dangerous Class*, Rev. ed. London: Bloomsbury.
Struck-Peregończyk, Monika. 2015. "Młode osoby niepełnosprawne na rynku pracy." Warszawa ASPRA.

Struck-Pergończyk, Monika. 2017. "Niepełnosprawność, młodość a aktywność zawodowa w świetle badań dotyczących młodych osób niepełnosprawnych w województwie podkarpackim." *Acta Universitatis Lodziensis. Folia Sociologica* 60: 87–110.
Turner, David M., and Daniel Blackie. 2018. *Disability in the Industrial Revolution: Physical Impairment in British Coalmining, 1780–1880*. Manchester, UK: Manchester University Press.
Wierzbicka-Wiszejko, Dorota. 2008. *Od samoakceptacji do aktywności? Postawy wobec własnej niepełnosprawności a aktywność zawodowa*. Warszawa: Academica Wydawnictwo SWPS.
World Health Organization. 1980. *International Classification of Impairments, Disabilities and Handicaps (ICIDH)*. Geneva, Switzerland: World Health Organization.
World Health Organization. 2001. *International Classification of Functioning (ICF), Disability and Health: Introduction*. Geneva, Switzerland: World Health Organization.

CHAPTER 4

Good Practices as a Tool for Modelling Employer Policies from the Open Labour Market

Abstract This chapter consists of two parts. In the first part, we discuss the functions of the organisation's personnel policy in relation to disabled employees, we analyse international documents regarding disability management in the workplace, as well as CSR and diversity management issues. In the second part, several key questions are considered, namely: what is a good practice in the field of employment of people with disabilities? Where does it come from? Why is it important for employers, employees and the society at large? We also briefly consider several examples of reports devoted to good practices.

Keywords Diversity management · Corporate social responsibility · Disability management · Good practices at work

1 THE IMPORTANCE OF HUMAN RESOURCES MANAGEMENT IN RELATION TO PEOPLE WITH DISABILITIES

1.1 Functions of Human Resources Policy

Personnel issues were always important for the development of modern organisations, although the scope of activities and functions changed. Initially, this area was referred to as "personnel administration". Staff administration, which emerged as a clearly defined field in the 1920s,

© The Author(s) 2020
E. Giermanowska et al., *Employing People with Disabilities*,
https://doi.org/10.1007/978-3-030-24552-8_4

largely dealt with technical aspects of employment. The personnel function in most organisations consisted in supporting management in the field of recruitment, general and time discipline, payroll system, training and storage of personal files (McKenna and Beech 1995, p. 2). Usually, it did not focus on the relationship between different employment practices and the overall results of the organisation. There was also a single paradigm in this area. Following the World War Two, a wider range of instruments was included in human resources management, taking into consideration pay administration, basic training and advice on relations between employers and employees. Since the 1970s, there has been an increase in the number of personnel involved in staffing. It was connected with the quantitative increase and expansion of legal solutions, as well as with a definite lack of labour supply on the market. The practice of personnel management to a large extent included activities related to recruitment, selection, training and payroll system (McKenna and Beech 1995, pp. 2–3).

Since the 1960s, European countries have witnessed increasing acceptance of the right of disabled people to work, in particular to employment in ordinary workplaces and on the open labour market. This was related to activities of social movements combating discrimination and with anti-discrimination legislation, including legislation on employment. Countries such as: Denmark, Finland, Portugal, Sweden and the UK began to base their policy on the employment of disabled persons on the right to work and the prohibition of discrimination (Garbat 2012, p. 90). The states stimulated the employment of disabled people, trying to make employers aware of the duty of solidarity with these people and the need to help the state solve the problem of unemployment. On the other hand, increasing emphasis has been put on preparing disabled people for work, providing them with high professional qualifications so that they could compete with non-disabled workers. At the same time, a high level of rehabilitation services, vocational education and the necessary specialist equipment were guaranteed (Garbat 2012, p. 90).

In the 1980s, personnel management entered a new phase of development. The human resource management concept developed in response to a significant increase in competitive pressure in business organisations as a result of processes such as globalization, deregulation and rapid technological change. These pressures increased the interest of companies in engaging in strategic planning and adapting various elements of the organisation to achieve organisational effectiveness. Despite the similarities between the management of personnel and the management of human resources, significant differences are emphasized in the literature on the subject. The distinctive features of HRM are: strategic integration (matching company strategy and HRM strategy), culture management (defining missions and values, strengthening them through communication, training and management processes through effects), engagement (gaining employees for the mission and the value of the organisation), total quality management, investing in human capital and a monolithic philosophy, meaning that the interests of the managerial staff and employees are convergent (Armstrong and Taylor 2014, p. 4).

The HR policy expresses a specific philosophy of the organisation and its values. It includes among others equal opportunities policy and diversity management (Armstrong and Taylor 2014). A comprehensive review of literature and research on HRM shows that equality and diversity issues play a key role in the development of personnel functions in modern organisations. Equality means "ensuring individuals or groups of individuals are treated fairly and equally and no less favourably, specific to their needs, including areas of race, gender, disability, religion or belief, sexual orientation and age" (Ahammad 2017, p. 418). Promoting equality should remove discrimination in all these areas. Bullying, harassment and victimization are also considered issues of equality and diversity. On the other hand, diversity aims "to recognise, respect, and value people's differences, to contribute and realise their full potential by promoting an inclusive culture for all staff and students" (Ahammad 2017, p. 418). The best ways to promote equality and diversity are as follows (Ahammad 2017, p. 418):

1. Treating all staff fairly;
2. Creating an inclusive culture for all employees;
3. Ensuring equal access to opportunities to enable employees to fully participate in the learning process;
4. Enabling all staff to develop their full potential;
5. Equipping staff with the skills to challenge inequality and discrimination in their work/study environment;
6. Making certain that any learning materials do not discriminate against any individuals or groups;
7. Ensuring that policies, procedures, and processes do not discriminate any one.

Equality and diversity issues have become central to an integrated European labour market. In the practice of human resources management, the laws on employment and social affairs have gained importance. Solutions in the areas such as improving working conditions, fair remuneration, equal opportunities, workforce mobility, trade union representation, employees' access to information, their involvement, and health and safety at work must take matters related to equality and diversity into account (McKenna and Beech 1995).

1.2 International Documents on Disability Management in the Workplace

Over the past few decades, a change in the approach to perception of disabled people and their social participation, including their participation in professional activity, clearly emerged. This was reflected in many international and national documents that we wrote about in Chapter 2. In this part, we will point to international documents regarding the management of people with disabilities in the workplace.

One such document is the "ILO code of practice: Managing disability in the workplace" developed by the International Labour Organization. The code was finalized and unanimously adopted at the tripartite meeting of experts in Geneva, 3–12 October 2001 (ILO 2002). For many years, ILO has been promoting the economic protection of people with disabilities, which can be achieved by their greater participation in professional activity. The right to work and the importance of economic independence on which international labour standards are based have been recorded in ILO Convention No. 159 on Vocational Rehabilitation and Employment (Disabled Persons), 1983, and its accompanying Recommendation No. 168. The current provisions are contained in United Nations Convention on the Rights of Persons with Disabilities, discussed in Chapter 2, which entered into force on 3 May 2008.

The purpose of developing the Code was to give practical guidance to employers of large, medium or small enterprises in the private or public sector, in developing and highly industrialized countries, on the adoption of a positive disability management strategy in the workplace. Disability management has been defined as "A process in the workplace designed to facilitate the employment of persons with a disability through a coordinated effort and taking into account individual needs, work environment, enterprise needs and legal responsibilities" (ILO 2002, p. 4).

The strategy of disability management in the workplace, according to the ILO recommendations, should be an integral part of the general employment policy of employers, specifically as part of the human resources development strategy. The disability management strategy should include provision for (ILO 2002, p. 10):

a. *recruiting jobseekers with disabilities, including those who have not worked before and those who wish to return to work after a period of non-employment;*
b. *equal opportunity for employees with disabilities;*
c. *job retention by employees who acquire a disability.*

The document adopted at the level of the workplace must be in accordance with national legislation, policy and practice. Its provisions should be created in cooperation with employee representatives, in consultation with individual employees with disabilities, occupational health services and, where possible, with organisations of people with disabilities. It is advisable to consult competent authorities and specialized agencies with expertise in issues related to disability. Important personnel procedures in developing the strategy are: recruitment, promotion, job retention and adjustments.

Recruitment. The implementation of the principle of equal opportunities in the recruitment process for disabled and non-disabled candidates is supported by the following activities on part of the employers: encouraging people with disabilities to submit applications, disseminating information about vacancies in the press, radio, Internet, cooperation with employment services for the disabled or other specialist agencies, adaptation of qualification tests and criteria for the selection of candidates to the requirements of a particular job, taking into account its accessibility for people with disabilities.

Employment of a disabled employee may be preceded by an internship, employment for a trial period or supported employment. They give the employer a chance to assess the abilities and capabilities of a disabled employee, make appropriate adjustments to the workplace and decide on further employment. In the process of adaptation to work, it is important to familiarize a new employee with the workplace, work environment, position and any adjustments related to disability.

Promotion. The policy of equal opportunities in the workplace also involves gaining the skills and professional experience necessary for further professional career. Dissemination of information about promotion opportunities and training in forms accessible to people with various types of disabilities is conducive to greater activity of disabled people in the pursuit of professional promotion.

Job Retention. An important element of the strategy is measures undertaken for workers who became disabled during employment. Employers should make it easier for such an employee to maintain employment or return to work by presenting him or her with various options. If it is impossible to return to the same job without making changes, one should carry out the necessary adjustments related to the work, workplace or work environment or transfer the employee to another position in the company. Personal counselling, rehabilitation and retention programmes support employment.

Adjustments. In some cases, adaptation of the workplace enabling effective work performance is a required condition for employing and retaining people with disabilities. This applies to the improvement of the accessibility of workspace, proper marking and information, adaptation of the workstation, tools and equipment enabling optimal work performance, as well as flexibility of the work schedule. To this end authorities should provide incentives for employers and support services.

The development of the discussed document at the level of the workplace should contribute to raising the awareness of all employees of the organisation. An important element of implementing the strategy is to provide employees with knowledge about disability issues in the workplace and overcoming stereotypes and prejudices that may arise in relation to the prospect of cooperation with people with disabilities.

Another document referring to the promotion of good practices in the employment of people with disabilities is the *Code of Good Practice for the Employment of People with Disabilities* adopted by the Bureau of the European Parliament of 22 June 2005. The aim of the document is "to provide a clear statement of the European Institutions' policy in relation to the employment of people with disabilities and ensure that all staff in the European Institutions comply with their legal and statutory obligations under anti-discrimination provisions and carry out their duties in a manner which is consistent with good equal opportunities practice" (2005: Article 1). Its adoption was preceded by consultations on improving the working conditions and career prospects of people with disabilities, which suggested that a more proactive approach should be taken to implement, evaluate and monitor the pre-existing Code of

Good Practice (2000 and revised in 2003), and that increased involvement of disabled staff members should be taken into account.

By accepting the aforementioned document, the European Institutions were obliged to ensure equal access to employment in the European Public Service. The importance of providing reasonable accommodation to meet the needs of people with disabilities and Parliament's needs was emphasized, and it was pointed out that it is up to the Institutions to prove that ensuring necessary accommodation imposes an unreasonable burden. Improvements can apply to all employment areas: recruitment, selection and appointment, career development, training, and promotion, transfers or any other employment benefit, social relationships within the Institutions. Accommodation is also a way of changing the workplace and may include: job redesign, purchasing or modifying equipment, flexible working arrangements.

Further articles contain a set of recommendations covering such elements of the personnel process as: recruitment, careers, working environment, information and awareness training, monitoring. The key element of the implementation of the described Code of Good Practice is continuous monitoring of its operation and improvement of the application of the introduced procedures. To this end, special services have been set up: the Equal Opportunities Service and the Interservice Working Party on the Accessibility of People with Disabilities.

The implementation of good practices related to the employment of disabled people in companies and institutions raises many basic questions about the reasons for employing people with disabilities. Some employers point to skills and talents as causes, others to the process of internalization of disability as a natural business practice. The reasons, however, are more complex, and low employment rates of disabled people emphasize that these questions are very important in modern societies. ILO analyses indicate several factors that interact with each other, which determine the employment of disabled people (Business as unusual: Making workplaces inclusive of people with disabilities ILO 2014, p. 9):

- Corporate social responsibility (initiatives on disability inclusion and projects related to people with disabilities);
- Personal commitment from the founder or the CEO of the company;
- Financial incentives (grants to compensate for expenses linked to reasonable accommodation, particularly important for small and medium enterprises);

- Pressure from society (pressure from other companies and organisations is increasing, including data protection officers and non-governmental organisations acting for the benefit of people with disabilities);
- Legislation (which is usually the most relevant initial driver).

In the following paragraphs, we will pay special attention to the occurrence of these factors in the organisational solutions and practices of the organisation.

1.3 Diversity Management and CSR

Corporate social responsibility (CSR) as an idea and practice originated in the USA. In the EU, this idea was popularized in phases (Csillag et al. 2018). Along with political and sociocultural changes, the problems faced by entrepreneurs have changed. While in the 1970s, the focus was on the safety and functionality of products, in the 1980s of the twentieth century, the negative external effects of companies' actions began to be discussed. In the 90s of the twentieth century, the effects of globalization were recognized and attention was paid to ecological issues, human rights and the activities of large corporations. Since the mid-1990s, business initiatives known as CSR have intensified. Csillag et al. (2018) distinguish three basic stages in this period:

- 1993–2001 as the first stage of awareness raising and practical initiatives in the field of CSR in Europe; many consulting companies supporting business in CSR were established and companies included such activity in their business model;
- 2001–2011, when EU initiatives (including "Green Paper: Promoting a European Framework for CSR" 2001) accelerated the implementation of the CSR idea in enterprises. Definitional unification of CSR took place in the EU and a discussion about the faces of CSR was established. The 2008 crisis undermined the stability of companies and limited their financial resources. At the same time, it made CSR an extremely important mechanism of self-regulation in the business sphere.
- Period after 2011: the European Commission has published a new CSR strategy; "CSR and social entrepreneurship as a way out of the crisis." "In Enterprise 2020 (CSR Europe, 2011), which is a main

part of Europe 2020 strategy CSR is handled as a tool for achieving intelligent, sustainable and inclusive growth. They invited all member states to create their own CSR action plan by 2014 and drew up a plan for installing mandatory non-financial reporting (as a continuation of the 2005 conception on CSR performance evaluation)" (Csillag et al. 2018, p. 67).

In post-transformational countries, CSR is a relatively new business orientation, as business was initially focused on the accumulation of economic profits, omitting the consequences of its activities for the social sphere and the natural environment.

The idea of CSR refers to building and maintaining positive relationships between companies and stakeholders, which include clients, suppliers, media, employees and social partners. Companies conducting their business take into account their impact on the external and internal environment of the organisation. The growing popularity of the CSR idea results from the synergistic relationship of three types of factors: the promotion of the idea of sustainable development by international organisations; social pressure to preserve the safe living conditions of people and to promote the practice of self-regulation of business, that is, the companies go beyond standard and routine activities (Karwacka 2008, pp. 97–98). In this context, the term corporate citizenship appears as a kind of citizenship of enterprises that consciously bear responsibility for their actions.

However, reports from practitioners and researchers indicate that the majority of CSR programmes are not strategic and companies practice different activities (Rangan et al. 2015). These programmes are often dispersed and uncoordinated. Rangan et al. (2015) analysing companies from various industries and geographical areas, distinguished three basic areas of activities in the field of CSR:

- Charitable activities: these programmes do not bring economic improvement to enterprises, but they satisfy important needs of the wider social environment;
- Company's operational efficiency improvement programmes: programmes within the existing business model that may increase the company's incomes in the long term as a result of solving an important social problem, e.g. investing in improving working conditions, health protection of employees and their families, especially in countries with low level of public health protection;

- Programmes resulting from the new business model that initiate a new type of company activity to solve social and environmental problems; usually, they are narrowly tailored programmes for a specific market segment or production line.

It is not possible to run uniform programmes in all forms, because they depend on the industry and the sector of the economy in which the entrepreneur operates, from the external company environment and the conditions of the geographic and natural environment in which companies operate, and on the motivation of people who work for them, direct and supervise them. In companies that care about CSR activities, CSR is usually compatible with the company's business mission, expresses its values and distinguishes it from enterprises focused on shareholder profits. In this way, companies gain a competitive advantage.

Business activities for people with disabilities can appear on each of the following CSR levels: from charitable activities (such as the funding of specialist instruments for school education for young people with disabilities), to operational programmes (e.g. implementing training in transport logistics security to reduce accidents employees suffer and take care of their health prophylaxis and rehabilitation) to a new business model (such as the creation of specialized jobs for disabled people based on the development of products or services targeted for this group of customers). An example of the development of a new business model is the activity of Bank Millennium in Poland, which introduced e-government services (contacts with social security institutions or treasury institutions) within e-banking, blind, hearing impaired or wheelchair users friendly (Jarzębska, n.d.). At the same time, the current business model has been improved by implementing the principles of accessibility to bank branches, the use of appropriate ATMs and adaptation of customer service services. These activities can also be described as Corporate Shared Value (CSV) strategy, where attempts to broaden the group of clients were accompanied by caring for their specific needs.

Analysis of the literature on the subject by Csillag et al. (2018) regarding CSR in the context of people with disabilities indicates a poor representation of this issue in the general material referring to CSR or disability itself. Researchers pointed out that such references could be encountered in discussions regarding diversity management, anti-discrimination activities or inclusion of disadvantaged groups into the labour market, which is particularly evident after 2000. Some authors of the analysed materials also point to the economic and moral context of CSR activities. For example, topics of business ethics and the importance of cultural factors in relation to CSR activities oriented at people with disabilities are considered. In contrast, Csillag et al. (2018, p. 77) on the example of two Hungarian cases, make an interesting observation that despite the holistic combination of human rights and fighting with discrimination at the international level, these two issues in the national level can be treated separately and in a non-complementary way. They also emphasize the importance of diffusion of good practices in the international approach and CSR reporting standards, the need to include the employment of people with disabilities into the whole of HRM procedures and the involvement of personnel departments in this area.

Despite the relative poverty of professional literature on CSR regarding people with disabilities and the lack of spectacular examples in this area, in recent years an interesting idea of CSR-D, i.e. the combination of CSR and disability has appeared. Currently, there are not many international positions that are devoted to CSR-D and its standards (Mazur 2016). In practice, this idea is actively promoted by the Spanish ONCE Foundation. It prepared a document called "CSR-D Guide Corporate Social Responsibility and Disability" (available at http://rsed.fundaciononce.es/en/prologos.html). It is a guide on how to include disabled people in CSR strategies of companies. The ONCE Foundation emphasizes that disabled people are significant stakeholders as potential and real employees, clients or pressure groups. Caring for disabled persons means also taking care of the company's image and its recognition as a socially committed and responsible organisation in the era of increasing interest of countries and international institutions in matters of disability. "The inclusion of the disability aspect in CSR has an influence on the company's policy in general, including commitments, actions and practices that go beyond social action. Disability can be part of several CSR areas such as government, investment policy, transparency, human resources, relationship with clients and providers, etc." (*CSR-D Guide Corporate Social Responsibility and Disability*, accessed on 2 February 2019). Acting according to CSR-D rules means:

- Equality of treatment and non-discrimination;
- Integration in the labour market as an element of value;
- Fostering full accessibility;

- Relationships with suppliers and subcontractors;
- Social action;
- Communication as a responsible tool.

Activities related to fulfilling the CSR-D standards recommendations are voluntary because socially responsible initiatives of companies should be undertaken voluntarily as a conscious commitment. Therefore, the key factor in the process of creating the above standards is the non-obligatory "auto-standardization", which does not use hard tools and does not enforce the law (Mazur 2016). Sociocultural aspects are important. The companies operate as allowed by the broadly defined external environment, which is confirmed by observations of Polish companies (Barczyński 2015). The observations revealed the reluctance of some entrepreneurs to publicize information on the employment of disabled people. This was connected with the fear of products or services of such companies labelled as of lower quality (as produced by people with disabilities). The unfavourable media climate, which was due to numerous irregularities in the use of public financial support dedicated to the employment of disabled people in the early 1990s, was also discouraging. Employment of people with disabilities was treated by entrepreneurs as a "promotional ballast" (Barczyński 2015, p. 25).

In promoting social responsibility, "diversity teams" often help companies, ensuring that the prohibition of discrimination is respected and that employees' talents are developed regardless of the socio-demographic characteristics of the employed. The relational dimension of CSR activities emphasizes the need to conduct a proper personnel policy that will ensure a satisfactory standard of living for employees and their professional development, appropriate organisational culture and internal communication within the company. Entrepreneurs began to take notice of diversity after many lawsuits filed against large corporations at the end of the twentieth century (mainly in the United States) for unequal treatment of employees (Dobbin and Kalev 2016). Unfortunately, modern programmes to combat prejudices and increase diversity often refer to practices used in the 1960s and have low effectiveness in the fight against stereotypes. Sociologists Frank Dobbin and Alexandra Kalev (2016) indicate that they are based mainly on controlling the behaviour of managers and shaming them with imposed rules or with the help of re-education programmes. Meanwhile, the most effective programmes to promote diversity engage managers in working for diversity; they enable them to have more intense professional contacts with representatives of minority groups, diversified by gender, age or disability. They use the natural need of managers to build a positive image in the eyes of others. Voluntary training, cross-training, participation in special task teams for diversity, participation in programmes aimed at recruiting employees from minority groups or mentoring are considered to be more effective tools (Dobbin and Kalev 2016).

Although disability is a fundamental dimension of diversity in organisations (in addition to gender, nationality, age, sexual orientation or ethnic origin), still—as shown by the analysis—there is "the conflict between disability and the ableist business case for diversity management has contributed to a limited attention to disability within diversity management practice and diversity management research" (Thanem 2008, p. 589). It is connected with the focus on the economic aspects of employing disabled people (profit/loss analysis), omitting social aspects. In the meantime, it is necessary to conceptualize practical and research initiatives with regard to general management and organisation issues, including (but not exclusively) the issue of diversity management. Attention should be paid to both the organisational level and the social practices of groups and individuals. In a situation where there is a risk of the diversity management programme being reduced for economic reasons, this problem of diversity may be additionally excluded from the organisation due to social norms of the dominant group or the individual perspective of perceiving the disabled body in relation to one's own body. According to Thanem (2008, p. 591), "more research is needed to understand the role of an underlying ableism in excluding disability from diversity management practices". "Ableism refers to ideas, practices, institutions, and social relations that presume able-bodiedness, and by so doing, construct persons with disabilities as marginalized, oppressed, and largely invisible 'others'" (Chouinard 1997, p. 380), that remind us of our vulnerability, fragility and death. "Ableism favors certain abilities that are projected as essential. Any deviation from or lack of these abilities is seen as a diminished state of being" (Hirschberg and Papadopoulos 2016, p. 3). The aptitude privilege is connected with ableism, which results from the conviction that certain benefits (advantages) can be gained only when having certain abilities necessary to acquire these benefits. This results in standards established in society.

Nanna Mik-Meyer (2016) Danish research indicates the importance of ableism as a norm that could hinder the introduction of diversity management programmes. The research deals with a discursive analysis of co-workers' construction of colleagues with visible impairments. Co-workers of disabled people spontaneously "included" (classified) workers with visible impairments into a group of people broadly defined as "other" (i.e. transvestites, non-ethnic Danes, homosexuals). It illustrates the strength of the norm of a functional body and the strength of the ableist discourse. The functioning discourse of inclusiveness/ tolerance in work organisations blocked discussions about the dissimilarity of persons with visible impairments (for fear of being accused of intolerance). Othering of workers with visible disability "creates contradictory discourses of ableism (which automatically produce difference) and tolerance and inclusiveness (which automatically render it problematic to talk about difference)" (Mik-Meyer 2016, p. 16). It gave rise to ambivalent attitudes of co-workers.

Organisations must therefore not so much fight against intolerance/ discrimination on the basis of prohibitions, but make people more sensitive and aware of the power of commonly accepted simplifications about the world. Making workers more sensitive by acting and experiencing the world as "others" is a more effective tool to promote diversity in the workplace than the next anti-discriminatory training of managers. The Polish branch of the international construction company SKANSKA has introduced such an initiative with great success. With the participation of the non-governmental organisation of people with disabilities (integration foundation), the company organized a city game, which was a lesson of architectural accessibility. All employees and co-workers of the company, from directors and presidents, through designers and architects, playing the role of people with various disabilities, have learned how difficult it is for people with disabilities to move around in urban space and what they should change in their projects to create a friendly public space and improve the living conditions of people with disabilities (Kałużna, n.d.).

Organisations employing people are increasingly aware of the importance of capturing talents in the labour market and taking care of their development. For example, several Silicon Valley companies took action encouraging the employment and development for workers with autism spectrum disorder (ASD) (Mickahail and Andrews 2018). Corporations such as SAP and Google have launched special recruitment and training programmes to hire and retain people with ASD at work. These companies appreciated the merits of Neuro-diversity due to the innovativeness of the different way of thinking and learning of employees with ASD (see Racław and Szawarska 2018). "People with ASD can be valuable creative assets for technology companies, in the coming years" (Mickahail and Andrews 2018, p. 149). Specific personality traits or ways of functioning of people with a particular type of disability turn out to be an asset in many industries and sectors. In an innovative project in Poland people with Down's syndrome were employed, within a mentorship programme, as employees supporting the staff of a social care home (nursing home) for the elderly. The characteristics of persons with Down's syndrome, i.e. slowness, lack of competitiveness, lack of competitive spirit, empathy, routine and operation have turned out to be necessary in working with older people and contact with people with Down was enriching for nursing home residents (Zakrzewska-Manterys 2015, p. 20).

At the same time, the focus on the diversity of employee teams requires HR specialists to take an innovative approach to the tools used in personnel management. Noticing the difference and working on fulfilling legal anti-discrimination standards alone does not protect against the creation of hidden inequalities in the workplace. This was demonstrated by Anne Cockayne (2018) on the example of employees with Asperger's Syndrome (AS), who experienced difficulties due to attempts to adapt to neurotypical norms, imposed by the majority. Their way of functioning and traits may not only negatively affect promotion and remuneration (among others due to problems with so-called social competences). Sometimes they become the reason for over-exploitation on the part of employers, using the tendency of AS people to work long hours with low pay and according to a very strict management style. At present, the creation of effective diversity management strategies requires interdisciplinary research and a multi-perspective approach of HR specialists in order to be able to solve the practical problems of individuals in the workplace regarding their identity and difference/diversity (Villesèche et al. 2018).

The diversity of employees can be considered to be both a challenge, in that it demands certain flexibility from the employer, and a source of new opportunities and possibilities. For example, it can be used when promoting the company as a good employer, or when developing or marketing a product (Griffin 2013, pp. 231–232). Indeed, diversity management became an important part of building the image of the company as an employer, in the process of employer branding, which is a process of branding "the employment experience that the firm offers, and the 'customers' of this brand and product are prospective and current staff" (Moroko and Uncles 2009, p. 183). Effective employer branding demands long-term purposeful strategy aimed at shaping the image of the company in the awareness of employees and stakeholders (Backhaus and Tikoo 2004) and real changes in the recognition of the potential of its employees and their role in the company's success, and what follows changes in practices related to recruitment and retaining of a diverse workforce. One might argue that employer branding is a positive response to changing legal and social circumstances demanding greater awareness of diverse workforce. On the other hand, it might lead to negative consequences, where, for example, people with disabilities are treated instrumentally and employed for the sake of their disabilities, as it were for show, rather than for specific skills and knowledge that they might possess. That way the organisation appears to be following directives of non-discriminatory policy and diversity management but in fact its practices are a far cry from employee empowerment and participation of groups facing discrimination. We will return to this issue later on in the chapter.

Employer branding and diversity management are matters that require strategic planning and awareness of local values. Not everywhere the use of employees with disability in building a company image will be to the direct benefit of the company. Strong prejudices present in certain societies and cultures, alongside with harmful stereotypes about people with disabilities, might discourage clients from using the products or services of a given company, and it might also discourage able-bodied workers from joining the organisation. This of course does not mean that local cultural values should be an excuse for not employing people with disabilities or for hiding the fact. But it does mean that more careful planning in a longer time perspective and a certain level of risk. Companies, especially international ones, have an important role to play in changing organisations and thus societies for the better and the spread of good practices in human resource management.

Good image of the organisation, confirmed by HRM, CSR certificates or belonging to exclusive groups or networks of employers serves to attract talent. Organisations operating in the EU (both private companies and public or non-governmental organisations) that have opted for diversity management, may become signatories of the Diversity Charter. The Diversity Charter is a written commitment which is signed by organisations that oblige themselves to the introduction of equal treatment policy and diversity management, as well as active prevention of discrimination and mobbing in the workplace. It is an international initiative promoted by the European Commission. Thousands of companies, organisations and institutions have signed the Charter in 21 countries of EU. In 2010, European Commission created the EU Platform of Diversity Charters that offers a place for existing European Diversity Charters to exchange and share experience and good practices more easily through Platform meetings, expert seminars and annual high-level forums (*EU Platform of Diversity Charters*, n.d.).

2 GOOD PRACTICES IN RESEARCH ON EMPLOYING PEOPLE WITH DISABILITIES

2.1 Definition of Good Practices

The concept of good practice emerged from the science of enterprise management. Already F. Taylor used the term "the one best way"— to point to the best way of doing something (Brajer-Marczak 2017, p. 16). Contemporary studies on good practices in managing organisation and organisational processes appeared in the 1980s, while a decade later, in connection with the development of the concept of New Public Management in public institutions good practices began to be identified with the public sector. There is no single valid definition of good practice. Krzysztof Rutkowski, following an analysis of materials available online, identified seven ways of understanding the term "good practices" (Rutkowski 2006, p. 3):

- The best way to do something,
- The most effective procedures and actions,
- Leading, i.e. giving competitive advantage and exemplary procedures and directions of action,
- Procedures and activities in a given business process that outweigh the results of competition,
- Formulas and procedures that ensured success in practice,
- Proven methodologies for consistent and effective business operations,
- Technique or reliable methodology in achieving the assumed results.

Certain definitions of good practices emphasize their innovative potential in introducing changes to the organisation and, hence, their usefulness. Others emphasize the uniqueness of processes described as good practices in achieving the best results of undertaken actions (Brajer-Marczak 2017, pp. 16–17). Following Renata Brajer-Marczak, as good practice, we define "an action that has brought concrete, positive results, that contains a certain element of innovation, is durable and reproducible, applicable in similar conditions elsewhere or by other entities. It is to provide the organization with the achievement of its business or non-business objectives" (Brajer-Marczak 2017, p. 17). In our opinion, social goals, aimed at achieving sustainable socio-economic development as part of CSR, will play an increasingly important role (see Rutkowski 2006).

In management and CSR literature authors often write on both good practices and best practices (the notion of best practice is also associated with certain management style in HR). While the connotation of both terms overlaps, these terms are not synonyms. So, for example, according to the Chevron approach, "a good practice is a technique, methodology, procedure, or process that has been implemented and has improved business results for an organization" while a best practice is "a good practice that has been determined to be the best approach for many organizations" (Jarrar and Zairi 2000, p. 735). As Armstrong and Taylor (2014, p. 24) points out, in the context of management, the idea of "best practice" has received a fair share of criticism for its claim of universality (e.g. Purcell 1999; Cappelli and Crocker-Hefter 1996; Boxall 2007). Different companies operate in different economic, legal, social and cultural circumstances and have access to different resources. It would therefore be somewhat idealistic to think that a good practice from one company can be effectively transferred in full to numerous other companies. Moreover, a practice can be judged as good using various criteria: economic profit, compliance with legal requirements, recommendations or standards, positive impact on company image, retaining of staff, etc. That is to be expected as companies have various aims and values. For those reasons, below we use a more neutral and humble notion of a "good practice". Another reason is that we do not want the reader to consider the case studies presented later on in the chapter as ready solutions to be easily transplanted into another setting. Any such transfer needs deep consideration, adaptation and an understanding of the internal logic of a practice and circumstances of its development. What is a good practice in one setting might not prove to be one in another setting, or yet again, with minor changes, it might make a lot of difference?

Enterprises are not the only setting in which best and good practices are spoken of. They are also present in the fields of medicine and education, where the term has a slightly different connotation. Although the present book deals with good practices in employment and is therefore closer to the field of management in its scope, it is worth considering, what the term "good practice" might imply in the context of so-called special education, in order to have a deeper understanding of wider implications of good practices. Just like in management there is no universal definition of good practice, but the term is used to refer to very diverse aspects of education: exemplary methodologies and strategies, effective educational and clinical processes, desirable student and client outcomes, integration potential, programme quality, transfer of values, etc. (Peters and Heron 1993, p. 372). Each of these elements raises further questions. What makes a methodology exemplary? What makes an educational process effective? What values do we want to transfer? What is a desirable outcome for a student or client, or indeed an employee? How do we measure integration and where? If these questions make the notion of a good practice even more remote or complicated, they do make one thing clear: good practices have consequences beyond the organisations that employ them. They have a direct impact on employees and their families, clients, and the society at large, but at the same time they are also shaped by those larger contexts. Because of that wider impact and context, when assessing good practices in employing people with disabilities, one must look beyond the direct benefits to the employer and consider those wider consequences.

Another area of practice, i.e. social work (including the sphere of support for people with disabilities) also provides many interesting conclusions. In the analysis of good practices in social work, the question of innovativeness as a feature of good practices is raised (Trawkowska 2014). First of all, it is stressed that the innovative character of a good practice is relative. It depends on the previous experience of a person, group or organisation. This means that innovation is evaluated due to the previous experience of the professional environment and the local environment in which good practices are created. Secondly, innovative action can be understood in two ways: as substantive innovation (models, methods, techniques, tools, labour standards) and as an organisational innovation (considered an interesting organisational solution).

In general, these two areas are interrelated, but organisational innovation (e.g. changes in the organisation structure) does not have to be accompanied by substantive innovation (in the content of procedures or methods of work of specialists)—and vice versa. Thirdly, good practice is directed at important problems of the present and related issues and interests; less so on future challenges. Fourthly, in order to be rooted in practice, it is necessary for good practice to be accepted by the professional community, or at least its opinion-forming part. As an organisational or substantive change, good practice should be reflected upon, argued and supported by scientific evidence, in relation to the consequences of transformations and not only the process/course of these changes (Trawkowska 2014, p. 14). It seems interesting to consider the effects of good HRM practices in relation to the wider social context, not just changes within the organisation, and to ask the question about the innovativeness of good practices in terms of a context (for whom? where?) in the personnel policy of the organisation employing people with disabilities.

Good practice in the field of employment of people with disabilities can be defined as a process, technique or innovation that serves better realization of company aims and improves the situation of people with disabilities in the workplace. A good practice preferably, has a universal character, that is a practice developed in one organisation should be easily transferred to another, but for reasons mentioned above it is not an essential characteristic.

What other characteristics then should be considered when developing good practices? In case of employing people with disabilities, one can look for inspiration across a very wide spectrum of literature, ranging from publications on human resource management, good practices in CSR and good practices in rehabilitation of people with disabilities. The following characteristics appear to be relevant (Karwińska and Wiktor 2008, p. 8) when identifying, or indeed developing, a good practice: effectiveness, efficiency, planning, reflexivity, innovation and compliance with ethical standards.

This list of characteristics, while extremely useful, when developing or transferring a practice, is not sufficient to explain why certain good practices related to employing people with disabilities work. As research shows the essential factor that makes such practices effective is the recognition by employers and their employees, that indeed, employing people with disabilities makes sense, and what follows, their desire to pursue that goal (Kotzian et al. 2014 a, b). In other words in order to develop a good practice related to employing people with disabilities, one must first want to employ them. This appears to be a necessary, though perhaps not sufficient, condition, for developing good practice in this area.

Organisations that achieve success through their good practices gain social legitimacy, attract resources and are likely to be imitated by other organisations. It does not mean of course that the transfer of good practices is going to be automatically successful. What works on one context, might not work in another, especially if we attempt to transfer a practice between different cultural and organisational setting. Nonetheless one might argue that good practices are likely to spread, not only through direct imitation, but all kinds of promotional activities, encouraging greater diversity among employees and greater employment rate of people with disabilities. However, when promoting and adopting good practices, one must keep their recipients in mind, their needs and abilities and the surrounding conditions (cultural, legal, institutional and political) that might have an impact on the success of a given good practice. One way of approaching the problem of adoption of good practices is to rely on benchmarking, that allows managers to compare and analyse good practices and creatively adopt them in a given setting.

2.2 Examples of Research Reports on Good Practices

As we have demonstrated so far, in recent years, the employment and equal treatment of people with disabilities became an important element of legislation related to employment, modern HR policies and positive company image. However, despite this, workers with disabilities, in comparison with able-bodied workers, are markedly underemployed. In order to combat this and aid the diffusion of good practices, a number of organisations prepare reports on existing good practices in the employment of workers with disabilities. The reports on good practices in this area present good practices among employers, but also, for example, in job centres or NGO's where the focus is not only the employment of disabled people, but their professional activation, or on particular solutions such as supported employment. These reports might be useful not only to entrepreneurs and employers, but also scientists researching the notion and practice of "good practices" in the area of employing disabled workers. Sometimes the focus of the report i good practices in the area of diversity at work, with disability being only one of the issues considered. There are also reports available on the employment of people with disabilities per se and related issues. These do not necessarily focus on good practices in business (although occasionally one might find mentions of there), but on the state of the employment and the problems in the area. All of these are useful in understanding the underlying issues and problems and in formulating solutions, but also all have some limitations.

One of the major problems when using these reports in research is that often they do not define what they mean by "good practices", and when they do, various definitions are used, which makes it difficult to compare the practices presented. Related to that is another problem, in that often the authors do not provide the selection criteria for presented good practices, and when they do, these also vary. Research methodology is often left out of the reports, which makes them less transparent to the readers.

In those reports that provide some sort of definition, criteria or core elements of good practice in the field of employment of people with disabilities, the focus of the definition is sometimes placed on the direct benefit of the person with disability (e.g. COWI 2011, p. 3; NDA 2018, p. 6; Kryńska 2013, p. 95). However, in other reports the importance of the wider context is recognized, in particular the benefit of the company employing people with disabilities (ILO 2010; Idström et al. 2013), and the importance of social structure, support system and values held by the society in implementing good practices (Idström et al. 2013). It is the second approach that we follow as researchers, as it must be recognized that workers with disabilities are part of a larger and complex whole, and if practices implemented with their decent employment in mind are to be successful, they have to successfully fit into the larger societal, organisational or legal structures.

An interesting question is who writes there reports and who funds the research that goes into their preparation and production. There are of course reports prepared by international organisations such as the ILO (e.g. Disability in the Workplace: Company Practices), or ILO in collaboration with WHO, state institutions such as National Disability Authority in Ireland (2010, Research on good practice in the employment of people with disabilities in the public sector) or, further afield, Australian Human Rights Commission (Willing to work, 2016), or reports prepared by trade Unions (e.g. Trade Union Conference UK. Disability and Work. A trade union guide to the law and good practice,

2011), to name a few. But what you often see in Europe are the results of various kinds of collaborations, usually funded by the EU or Norway grants. These collaborations are not only across sectors (such as education, trade unions, business, NGOs and self-government) but also across borders, and include a number of perspectives. That, we believe, is the result of the EU funding mechanisms and strategy that are to encourage international and inter-sectional dialogue, network building and collaboration, and promote greater social integration. Many of these documents report on activities and projects initiated and funded by the EU, including projects promoting the employment of people with disabilities. As author of one such report notes (Kryńska 2013), the risk associated with these initiatives is that they have limited time frame and funding, and the activities reported as good practice, are likely to cease once the funds run dry. Nonetheless in further studies of good practice, it might be worthwhile to consider several examples of such collaborations and their reports, in order to see how good practices are studied and presented. Below, we present several such examples.

i. **Diversity at Work, 2007**

This report, or rather a brochure, is the result of the collaboration between ETNO (European Telecommunications Network Operators) and UNI (an international confederation of trade unions) and was funded by the European Commission, DG Employment, Social Affairs and Equal Opportunities. And it reviews "Good Corporate Practices in the Telecoms Sector". Good practices are presented divided into groups associated with particular groups of workers (women, age, disability, sexual orientation, religion). There are also overview chapters on raising the awareness of equal opportunities for all and encouraging diversity. The report presents four very short examples of good practices involving disabled workers. Nowhere in the brochure are "good practices" defined. It is difficult to define the purpose of this document. On the one hand, it provided interesting examples of good practices; on the other, these are not rooted in larger contexts, we do not know how do they "click" with other elements such as local legislation, health care, infrastructure and culture. It is also interesting to ask who is the target audience for this document? Managers of the telecoms industry already employing some of these practices? Somebody from the outside? One cannot help, but feel that this was an element of a PR exercise. These issues draw attention to the fact that when reading reports on management practices, one must consider vested interests of parties involved in the creation of such documents.

ii. **Best Practices in the Field of Professional Activation of Disabled People in the Danish Labour Market, 2014 (Rosmus 2014)**

This report is the result of a collaboration between Polish job centre in Białystok and Danish partner Jobcentre Aarhus and was funded by the European Social Fund. It is a thorough presentation of the Danish practice in the area of professional activation of disabled people. It contains information on Danish economy, its strengths and weaknesses, labour market, the flexicurity system, the situation of people with disabilities on the labour market, relevant legislation and support systems (assistants, supported employment, sheltered jobs, etc.) and it also presents activities of the Jobcentre Aarhus in professional activation of disabled people, a chart of employment organisation and social issues in Aarhus. It contains details on how legislation on integration and social policy fits with particular organisation of labour support, benefit system and activities of the centre and matters related to labour market analysis, important for the centre's activities efficiency. All in all, it appears to be a thorough case study of the Danish model in action. However, given the collaborative nature of the project what appears to be missing is the analysis of the Danish case study with the view of transferring Danish good practices, which are deeply ingrained in local legislation and welfare state model and system of values, to Polish ground, or indeed anywhere else. This report does not even consider the question of the method of transfer of good practices that result from the state labour policy, and its regional (at the level of self government) interpretation and implementation. Which begs the question what was the purpose of the collaboration between Poland and Denmark in this case.

iii. **Best Practices for the Employment of People with Disabilities and Altered Working Capacity, 2016 (Németh 2016)**

This is a report prepared by a consortium consisting of Corvinus University of Budapest, Salva Vita Foundation, Türr István Training and Research Institute and NHO Service (Norway). It was financed through EEA Financial Mechanism, commonly referred to as Norway grants.

It presents examples of best practices in Hungary and in Norway in the area of employment of people with disabilities, and also in advocacy for their rights. Nowhere in the report are best practices defined, though occasionally their success is measured by the number of employees with disability the company has, and their retention rate. When reading the Hungarian examples, one is not always sure what the best practice exactly consists of, as the dominant focus in the examples is the employment of people with disabilities alone or activities on behalf of their professional activation.

One could definitely use more analysis and detail in the context of their originality, innovation, problems combated, despite the headings of "Difficulties, strengths, results and key success factors". We do not know what criteria were used to select the presented examples.

iv. Compendium of Good Practice. Supported Employment for People with Disabilities in the EU and EFTA-EEA, 2011

This report was prepared by COWI consulting group in association with Work Research Institute and European Union of Supported Employment and was financed by the EU. It stands out among other reports in that it presents its research methodology and defines criteria for classifying a practice as good, both of which increase its usefulness and credibility. The Compendium of Good Practice presents data that was gathered as part of a general study of supported employment for people with disabilities in the EU and EFTA-EEA. The original general study covered thirty countries, out of which six were selected for an in-depth study: Austria, Czech Republic, Norway, Spain, Sweden and the UK. It presents ten case studies of good practices of supported employment, in which a disabled worker found a job on the open labour market, based on information gained from, the disabled workers, the actual employers of those particular supported employees, as well as information from Service Providers and Job Coaches involved. The criteria for identifying a practice as good were the following (COWI 2011, p. 3):

- The disabled employee found the job through a supported employment service,
- There was an identifiable job coach involved,
- The disabled employee had attended the job for at least six months,
- The job was in the open labour market, there is a legal job contract and payment according to regulatory standards.

The criteria for identifying good practices are listed, which makes it easier for the reader to assess the effectiveness of a given practice and also makes the selection process more transparent. In addition case studies were selected to show a variety of different situations in terms of type of disability, age, gender, company size and branches, different geographical regions and different policy frameworks.

The fact that the report presents the perspectives of both employers and employees, aids better understanding of the functioning of particular solutions and their transfer to other contexts. Also the report puts particular examples of good practices related to supported employment in the context of local legislation and local organisation of support system which also places these solutions in a wider perspective.

The report, in its methodology section, also contains interview guides for interviewing job coaches, employers and employees, which is of use for those who either want to assess the presented data in greater depth, or adapt and repeat the study.

All in all, the report is good source of ideas and information about a specific solution in the area of employing people with disabilities, that is "supported employment", which by definition deals with a certain measure of cooperation between employers and providers of supported employment services. While employing disabled workers does not always involve supported employment, this report was inspiring in the design of our own study, in which, as we discuss in the next chapter, we wanted to deal with a wider range of good practices within the area of employment of people with disabilities.

In this chapter, we demonstrated how the notion of "good practices" is used in order to shape policies at the level of the state and individual employers, and how it is adapted in order to serve the interests of the companies involved (which may also include the interest of employees with disabilities themselves). Although the notion of "good practices" lacks a fixed and universal meaning, it inspires a number of activities that promote both it and the entities that employ or promote it, for example, through research or quasi-research activities. The fact that the meaning of "good practices" is open to interpretation implies a fair amount of flexibility. This in turn, as our analyses clearly show in the next chapter, may be turned to the advantage of both employer and employee with disability, or may bring more harm than good.

References

Ahammad, Taslim. 2017. "Personnel Management to Human Resource Management (HRM): How HRM Functions?" *Journal of Modern Accounting and Auditing* 13 (9): 412–420.

Armstrong, Michael, and Stephen Taylor. 2014. *Armstrong's Handbook of Human Resource Management Practice*, 13th ed. London: Kogan Page Limited.

Backhaus, Kristin, and Surinder Tikoo. 2004. Conceptualizing and Researching Employer Branding. *Career Development International* 9 (5): 501–517.

Barczyński, Andrzej. 2015. "Społeczna odpowiedzialność biznesu w zatrudnianiu osób z niepełnosprawnościami – idea a rzeczywistość." In *Ergonomia niepełnosprawnym. Aktywizacja zawodowa*, edited by Joanna Lecewicz-Bartoszewska and Aleksandra Polak-Sopińska, 7–28. Łódź: Wydawnictwo Politechniki Łódzkiej.

Boxall, Peter. 2007. "The Goals of HRM." *The Oxford handbook of human resource management*, 48–67. Oxford: Oxford University Press.

Brajer-Marczak, Renata. 2017. "Dobre praktyki w doskonaleniu procesów biznesowych." *Studia Informatica Pomerania* 1 (43): 15–24.

Business as Unusual: Making Workplaces Inclusive of People with Disabilities. 2014. Geneva: International Labour Office.

Cappelli, Peter, and Anne Crocker-Hefter. 1996. Distinctive Human Resources are Firms' Core Competencies. *Organizational Dynamics* 24 (3): 7–22.

Chouinard, Vera.1997. "Making Space for Disabling Difference: Challenges Ableist Geographies." *Environment and Planning D: Society and Space* 15: 379–390.

Cockayne, Anne. 2018. "The 'A' World Employment: Considerations of Asperger's Syndrome for HR Specialists." In *Hidden Inequalities in the Workplace: A Guide to the Current Challenges, Issues and Business Solutions*, edited by Valerie Caven and Stefanos Nachmias, 39–66. Cham: Palgrave Macmillan.

Code of Good Practice for the Employment of People with Disabilities, adopted by the Bureau of the European Parliament of 22 June 2005. Accessed February 25, 2019. http://www.europarl.europa.eu/pdf/disability/code_good_practice_en.pdf.

COWI. 2011. *Compendium of Good Practice: Supported Employment for People with Disabilities in the EU and EFTA-EEA*. Luxembourg: European Union.

Csillag Sára, Zsuzsanna Gyori, and Réka Matolay. 2018. "Two Worlds Apart? Corporate Social Responsibility and Employment of People with Disabilities." In *The Critical State of Corporate Social Responsibility in Europe*, 57–81. Published online: 20 June 2018. Permanent link to this document https://doi.org/10.1108/S2043-905920180000012003.

CSR-D Guide Corporate Social Responsibility and Disability. Accessed February 2, 2019. http://rsed.fundaciononce.es/en/prologos.html.
Dobbin, Frank, and Alexandra Kalev. 2016. "Why Diversity Programs Fail?" *Harvard Business Review* 94 (7, July–August): 52–60.
ETNO. 2017. "Diversity at Work." Accessed March 30, 2019. https://etno.eu//downloads/reports/brochure_diversity_uk_final.pdf.
EU Platform of Diversity Charters. Accessed October 6, 2018. https://ec.europa.eu/info/policies/justice-and-fundamental-rights/combatting-discrimination/tackling-discrimination/diversity-management/eu-platform-diversity-charters_en.
Garbat, Marcin. 2012. *Zatrudnianie i rehabilitacja zawodowa osób z niepełnosprawnością w Europie*. Zielona Góra: Oficyna Wydawnicza Uniwersytetu Zielonogórskiego.
Griffin, Ricky W. 2013. *Fundamentals of Management*. Mason: South-Western Cengage Learning.
Hirschberg, Marianne, and Christian Papadopoulos. 2016. "'Reasonable Accommodation' and 'Accessibility': Human Rights Instruments Relating to Inclusion and Exclusion in the Labor Market." *Societies* 6 (3): 1–16.
Idström Anna, Marko Stenroos, and Minna Uimonen, eds. 2013. *Decent Work: Promising Practices in the Employment of People with Disabilities from Sweden, Denmark, Estonia, and Finland*. Helsinki: ASPA.
ILO. 2002. *Managing Disability in the Workplace: ILO Code of Practice*. Geneva: International Labour Office.
ILO. 2010. *Disability in the Workplace: Company Practices*. Geneva: International Labour Office.
Jarrar, Yasar F., and Mohamed Zairi. 2000. Best Practice Transfer for Future Competitiveness: A Study of Best Practices. *Total Quality Management* 11 (4–6): 734–740.
Jarzębska, Iwona. n.d. "Społeczna odpowiedzialność wpisana w usługi banku." Accessed October 5, 2018. https://www.hbrp.pl/b/spoleczna-odpowiedzialnosc-wpisana-w-uslugi-banku/PKBXzUn4Z.
Kałużna, Ewelina. n.d. "Park dla wymagających." Accessed October 10, 2018. https://www.hbrp.pl/b/park-dla-wymagajacych/Fg3G41bW.
Karwacka, Marta. 2008. Relacja pracodawca-pracownik w kontekście realizowania idei społecznej odpowiedzialności biznesu (CSR). In *Partnerstwo - Rodzina - Równość - Praca. Godzenie życia zawodowego i rodzinnego jako wyzwania dla polityki społecznej - doświadczenia z realizacji projektu PIW EQUAL*, edited by Krzysztof Piątek and Arkadiusz Karwacki, 91–102. Toruń: Wydawnictwo Naukowe Uniwersytetu Mikołaja Kopernika.
Karwińska, Anna, and Dobrosława Wiktor. 2008. "Przedsiębiorczość i korzyści społeczne: identyfikacja dobrych praktyk w ekonomii społecznej." *Ekonomia społeczna. Teksty* 6: 7–8.

Kotzian, Joanna, Magdalena Pancewicz, and a team of consultants from HRK S.A. 2014a. "Rozdział I Praktyki polskie." In *Zatrudniając niepełnosprawnych. Dobre praktyki w Polsce i innych krajach Europy*, edited by Ewa Giermanowska, 117–216. Kraków: Akademia Górniczo-Hutnicza im. S. Staszica w Krakowie.

Kotzian, Joanna, Magdalena Pancewicz, and a team of consultants from HRK S.A. 2014b. Rozdział II Praktyki zagraniczne. In *Zatrudniając niepełnosprawnych. Dobre praktyki w Polsce i innych krajach Europy*, edited by Ewa Giermanowska, 217–294. Kraków: Akademia Górniczo-Hutnicza im. S. Staszica w Krakowie.

Kryńska, Elżbieta. 2013. *Dobre praktyki aktywizacji zawodowej osób z niepełnosprawnością realizowane przez organizacje pozarządowe w Polsce*. Warsaw: Instytut Pracy i Spraw Socjalnych.

Mazur, Michał. 2016. "Społeczna odpowiedzialność przedsiębiorstw a zatrudnienie osób niepełnosprawnych." PhD diss., University of Warsaw.

McKenna, Eugene, and Nic Beech. 1995. *The Essence of Human Resource Management*. London: Prentice Hall.

Mickahail, Bethany K., and Kate Andrews. 2018. "Embracing People with Special Needs and Disabilities." In *Diversity and Inclusion in the Global Workplace: Aligning Initiatives with Strategic Business Goals*, edited by Carlos Tasso Eira de Aquino and Robert W. Robertson, 139–152. Cham: Palgrave Macmillan.

Mik-Meyer, Nanna. 2016. "Othering, Ableism and Disability: A Discursive Analysis of Co-workers' Construction of Colleagues with Visible Impairments." *Human Relations*. First published online: February 4. https://doi.org/10.1177/0018726715618454.

Moroko, Lara, and Mark D. Uncles. 2009. Employer Branding and Market Segmentation. *Journal of Brand Management* 17 (3): 181–196.

National Disability Authority. 2018. "Research on Good Practice in the Employment of People with Disabilities in the Public Sector." Accessed March 30, 2019. http://nda.ie/Publications/Employment/Employment-Publications/Good-practice-in-employment-of-people-with-disabilities-in-the-public-sector1.pdf.

Németh, Ildikó, ed. 2016. *Best Practices for the Employment of People with Disabilities and Altered Working Capacity*. ProAbility project. Budapest: Corvinus University of Budapest.

Peters, Mary T., and Timothy E. Heron. 1993. When the Best is not Good Enough. *The Journal of Special Education* 26 (4): 371–385.

Purcell, John. 1999. Best Practice and Best Fit: Chimera or Cul-de-Sac? *Human Resource Management Journal* 9 (3): 26–41.

Racław, Mariola, and Dorota Szawarska. 2018. "Ukryte/niewidoczne niepełnosprawności a polityka tożsamości i etykietowania w życiu codziennym." *Przegląd Socjologii Jakościowej* 14 (3): 30–46.

Rangan, Kasturi, Lisa Chase, and Sohel Karim. 2015. "The Truth About CSR." *Harvard Business Review* 93 (1/2) (January–February): 40–49.

Rosmus, Magdalena. 2014. *Best Practices in the Field of Professional Activation of Disabled People in the Danish Labor Market.* Białystok: Wojewódzki Urząd Pracy w Białymstoku.

Rutkowski, Krzysztof. 2006. "Zrozumieć fenomen najlepszych praktyk w logistyce i zarządzaniu łańcuchem dostaw. Europejskie wyzwania projektu BestLog." *Gospodarka Materiałowa i Logistyka* 12: 2–7.

Thanem, Torkild. 2008. "Embodying Disability in Diversity Management Research." *Equal Opportunities International* 27 (7): 581–595. Permanent link to this document http://dx.doi.org/10.1108/02610150810904292.

Trawkowska, Dobroniega. 2014. "Czym są dobre praktyki w pomocy społecznej?" *Empowerment. O polityce aktywnej integracji* 1 (4): 9–16.

Villesèche, Florence, Sara Louise Muhr, and Lotte Holck. 2018. *Diversity and Identity in the Workplace: Connections and Perspectives.* Cham: Palgrave Macmillan.

Zakrzewska-Manterys, Elżbieta. 2015. "O projekcie "Pomocna Dłoń" i wsparciu w systemie mentorskim." In *Podręcznik dla zainteresowanych wprowadzaniem osób upośledzonych umysłowo na rynek pracy do sektora społecznego. Cz. I. Model wsparcia mentorskiego jako forma specyficznej aktywizacji zawodowej osób upośledzonych umysłowo*, 14–25. Warszawa: Stowarzyszenie Rodzin i Opiekunów Osób z Zespołem Downa "Bardziej Kochani".

CHAPTER 5

Good Practices in the Personnel Management Process

Abstract In this chapter, specific areas of human resources and diversity management are analysed together with related examples of good practices obtained from a research study carried out in 2012–2014. Here, we aim to demonstrate how good practices, most often developed by the employers, serve as a tool for modelling employer policies related to diversity management. We also consider negative consequences of mismanagement of good practices.

Keywords Diversity management · Disability management · Good practices at work · The negative side of good practices

1 Research Methodology

The study of good practices dealing with the employment of disabled people in Poland and Europe was carried out as part of the project on the state public policy towards disability, implemented in 2012–2014.[1]

---

[1] The project was led by prof. Barbara Gąciarz from the Faculty of Humanities at AGH in Kraków and financed by PFRON. The following persons were engaged in the research and data analysis: Ewa Giermanowska (ISNS UW), Joanna Kotzian (HRK S.A.), Magdalena Pancewicz (HRK S.A.), Magdalena Arczewska (ISNS UW), Mariola Racław (ISNS UW). The study uses information included in the publication of the research project: Giermanowska (2014a), including: Giermanowska (2014b, c), Kotzian et al. (2014a, b), Arczewska et al. (2014). The research results and data analysis were published

© The Author(s) 2020
E. Giermanowska et al., *Employing People with Disabilities*,
https://doi.org/10.1007/978-3-030-24552-8_5

The aim of the research module dealing with employment was gathering information and data analysis of programmes and practices recognized as good in companies and institutions of the open labour market. Good practice has been defined as a universal process, technique or innovation that involves the employment of disabled people and improves their situation at a given workplace, but also contributes to a better quality implementation of organisational goals. Empirical studies covered two types of research.[2] Qualitative research dealing directly with the functioning of good practices, based on the case study method, was carried out in ten companies/ institutions in Poland and ten in other European countries. Surveys, carried out in 100 companies and institutions in Poland employing people with disabilities, supplemented with qualitative interviews with employers from the open labour market, covered the employment conditions of employees with disabilities (Giermanowska 2014b). The latter research results and analyses regarding the opinions of employers on the employment situation of people with disabilities in Poland will not be presented in detail in the chapter, but they constitute a source of knowledge for the proposed conclusions.

In the further part of the chapter, we will focus on the results of research of good practice based on case studies approach. The selection of companies and institutions was made based on the analysis of documents and consultations with experts. The aim was to choose

---

in: Giermanowska (2014a). *Zatrudniając niepełnosprawnych. Dobre praktyki pracodawców w Polsce i innych krajach Europy*. Kraków: Akademia Górniczo-Hutnicza im. S. Staszica w Krakowie.

[2] In Poland: Altix (IT company, Warsaw), Carrefour Polska (retail chain, Warsaw), Sopockie Towarzystwo Ubezpieczeń Ergo Hestia (insurance/financial company, Sopot), Hutchinson (automotive company, Bielsko Biała), Dr Irena Eris Cosmetics Laboratory (cosmetics company, Piaseczno), Offices of Rehabilitation Rudek (medical care, Rzeszów), Sodexo (commercial real estate service, Warsaw). Municipal Public Library (Katowice), Office of the Ombudsman (Warsaw), State Plant Health and Seed Inspection Service—Central Laboratory (Toruń);

In Europe: Allehånde Køkken (restaurant company, Denmark), Ford-Werke GmbH (automotive company, Germany), IKEA Deutschland (retail company, Germany), Marionnaud Parfumeries (cosmetics company, France), Max Hamburgerrestauranger (restaurant company, Sweden), Rehab Station Stockholm (rehabilitation company, Sweden), Thales Group (arms industry, aerospace, land transport, France), Électricité Réseau Distribution France (energy company, France), European Parliament (Belgium/ Luxembourg), Department of Social Integration of People with Disabilities (Cyprus).

such employers, whose good practices in employing disabled people are recognized on the domestic market and even at the international level. Good practices were a source of knowledge for the authors of the project, but also a form of communication with employers. Hence, the project uses the knowledge and experience of consultants (from the HRK S.A. consulting company) who have direct contact with employers from the Polish and foreign labour market in the field of personnel recruitment and development, building the image of employers and social research. The added value of the implemented project was the joint participation of academic researchers and practitioners. Joanna Kotzian and Magdalena Pancewicz from the HRK S.A. played an active role in the preparation, implementation and analysis of the individual case studies.

Description and analysis of each case (company/institution) were made on the basis of available data and interviews and observations (where possible). The description of each company/institution uses information from the following sources:

- documents of the organisation: codes of ethics, organisational procedures for the management of diversity and disability in the workplace, training programmes in this regard;
- statistics of employment for people with disabilities;
- archive data: information on the origin of employment of disabled persons and practices in this field;
- internal physical artefacts: films, photos and websites;
- articles about the organisations dealing with the employment of disabled employees;
- applicable legislation and practices in a given country.

In each company/institution, interviews were carried out with representatives of employers and employees: direct (in Poland), telephone and Internet-based (in other countries), based on a scenario with prepared dispositions. Interviews were conducted with a representative of the board and/or the personnel department. In addition, in each case study, a description of an individual case (employed person) was made, based on an interview with the disabled person, her/his supervisor, co-worker and possibly subordinates. Interviews with a disabled employee, her/his supervisor and colleagues helped to show the social dimension of the organisational integration process. An additional source of information was direct observation by researchers (only in Poland).

Analysis of data from various sources (the so-called data triangulation method) permitted better understanding of the internal and external conditions of success of good practices. The proceedings in the course of research carried on case studies proved more difficult than expected by the authors. During the contact with foreign companies/institutions, non-governmental organisations proved to be very useful as they help the authors to reach these organisations. In the case of research conducted on the Polish labour market, it was difficult to obtain useful information from non-governmental organisations dealing with people with disabilities. They were reluctant to cooperate with private entities, treating them as competitors. Cooperation with public institutions also turned out not to be very effective. The questions addressed to them were most often passed on to other units, and response was delayed or often there was no response whatsoever.

Identification of companies and institutions for the study and the arrangements for the course of the study in individual organisations have proven to be the most difficult and the most labour-intensive stages of the project and contributed to the prolongation of the course of research. In addition, the extension of the duration of the research was caused by: unexpected absence of a disabled employee indicated for the study caused by his/her poor state of health, difficulties in finding time to conduct an interview (in the case of people in higher positions), no possibility of employee participation in the study during the hours of work, the need to hire a sign interpreter, the need to authorize transcriptions or notes on the interview and the authorization of the report. In the case of some countries, an additional difficulty was the applicable legal regulations, which obscure information about the employee's disability (such information is covered by medical confidentiality). The employer, wanting to take part in the study, had to wait for an employee to volunteer, as he could not indicate the person or ask her to participate in the study.

An important part of the project was the dissemination of its results. The results of the research were published in the monograph of the project (Giermanowska 2014a) and in numerous scientific articles, as well as popular science publications. A brochure, based on research results, was prepared for employers participating in research and sent to several dozen largest companies in Poland. The research results were presented at scientific and specialist conferences related to the HR area and with the participation of employers. Research results have been made available to public institutions responsible for employment of people with disabilities: State Fund for the Rehabilitation of the Disabled (PFRON), Ministry of Family, Labour and Social Policy (MRPiPS), Government Plenipotentiary for Disabled People. Unfortunately, the project results were not evaluated.

In the further part of the chapter, we will present selected personnel procedures, defined as good practices referring to the said research results. We will consider such issues as: recruitment and induction of an employee, adapting the workplace and assistantship, retaining the employee in employment and his development, managing disability issues in the workplace. In the end, we will also discuss the issues of employer's image in relation to disability and the dark side of good practices. In this part of the chapter, descriptions of specific practices of companies and institutions (in frames) will be based on selected fragments of analyzes prepared by Joanna Kotzian, Magdalena Pancewicz and a team from HRK S.A.

2 Recruitment and Induction

Organisation management consists in the optimal use of all its resources to achieve the set goals. People in the organisation are both a valuable resource and decision-makers about optimizing the use of all other resources of the organisation. The effectiveness of the organisation's operation depends on the productivity of its employees, which results from the adjustment of socio-demographic features to the organisational tasks set before them. On the other hand, a significant part of problems in organisations is generated by employees, and they are in turn solved by other staff members. As a strategic resource, people can creatively react to the opportunities and threats appearing before the organisation. The main purpose of the personnel policy is therefore to provide the organisation with the required number of suitably qualified employees at a specific place and time. In the situation of shortages in the labour force on the local labour market, with high competition from other organisations, finding candidates may be difficult and the unoccupied vacancy is generating real losses.

Organisations that have seen the potential of employees with disabilities as attractive job candidates are trying to create appropriate recruitment and selection procedures. They operate in accordance with the principle of non-discrimination and full accessibility that arise from acts of international or national law. It is worth emphasizing that a large part of the literature on employees with disabilities focuses on issues related to the initial stages of the employee's functioning in the organisation, mainly on recruitment and employee induction process (Paszkowicz 2009).

An overview of good practices indicates that the recruitment process in such organisations is characterized by:

- Non-application of generally separate recruitment practices in relation to able-bodied and disabled people, application of the principle of distinguishing the competencies and not the employment parity. The only exception was recruitment of employees with intellectual disability, when a legal guardian or job coach may be present during interviews. Similarly, a sign language interpreter may be present during interviews with deaf people.
- The use of specific recruitment channels, i.e. cooperation with non-governmental organisations helping disabled persons or associating disabled people, cooperation with public, private or non-governmental institutions preparing people with disabilities to work or intermediating in their employment.
- Signalling in press advertisements that the company/institution is a friendly environment for disabled people.
- Establishment of a special position or team for disability management policy, which elaborates the principles of external and internal recruitment.
- The use of pre-selection in the case of cooperation with institutions or organisations that are the source of disabled candidates for work.

An example: Cooperation between the Integralia Foundation and Sopot-based insurance company Ergo Hestia (Poland)

The beginnings of the employment of disabled people in Sopot Insurance Company Ergo Hestia are connected with the establishment of the "Integralia" foundation in 2004 (Ergo Hestia Group Foundation for the vocational integration of people with disabilities [Fundacja Grupy Ergo Hestia na rzecz integracji zawodowej osób niepełnosprawnych]). Then the management of Ergo Hestia Group decided that the company would start an active CSR policy, and the idea of the foundation was considered close to the company's values. During the research, the foundation employed 12 employees with moderate and severe disabilities and 4 employees without disabilities.

The main purpose of the foundation is to support people with disabilities at the start of their careers by organizing free trainings. The foundation also acts as a recruitment agency (it has an appropriate certificate), participates in job fairs, cooperates with universities, career offices and labour offices, thus acquiring disabled employees both for the needs of Ergo Hestia Group and other employers from all over Poland. Thanks to the cooperation of "Integralia" with companies representing various industries, people with various kinds and degrees of disability find jobs. Since 2009, the Volunteer Club has also been operating in the Ergo Hestia Group, as part of which the company's employees run workshops for the disabled (Kotzian et al. 2014a, pp. 139–140).

The approach offered by the Integralia Foundation is comprehensive. Workshops but also individual support meetings with specialists in the field of the labour market, career counselling, psychologists and coaches are organized. In the ERGO Hestia Group, there is a practice-oriented induction process for working in a corporation. They look for people with disabilities with the right competencies for various positions in the offices and departments of the Group. *"Such a person begins as an employee of the Integralia Foundation, but is delegated to work in the Group. This is an adaptation period, we diagnose areas for development. The foundation provides support in this area. We strive for the employee, to, after a period of two years, to work directly for a given office in ERGO Hestia out of his or her own initiative. Then the transition takes place on the principle of internal recruitment. In this manner, about 50 people found employment in our company. Through us, they can also go to other companies in the open labour market".* (Pomagają niepełnosprawnym znaleźć pracę. Z Darią Uljanicką, członkiem zarządu fundacji Integralia Grupy ERGO Hestia rozmawiała Anna Dobiegała 12 marca 2018, http://trojmiasto.wyborcza.pl/trojmiasto/7,35612,23120753,pomagaja-niepelnosprawnym-znalezc-prace.html, accessed 1.04.2019).

Ergo Hestia (insurance/financial industry, Poland)—the company carries out activities in the area of CSR—has set up a foundation for the integration of people with disabilities "Integralia" and engages employees in employee volunteering for people with disabilities. Sopot-based Ergo Hestia, as a partner of "Integralia", provides other employers with advice on how to employ people with disabilities (Giermanowska 2014c; http://www.integralia.pl/o-fundacji/, accessed 1.04. 2019).

> **An example: Recruitment and induction in the *Électricité Réseau Distribution France***

In recruitment, the company does not use job advertisements addressed only to people with disabilities. Every person with the required competences can be accepted for work; therefore, disability is not an asset or an obstacle. All candidates can respond to the advertisement as well as apply to work in the company through its website (https://selectra.info/energie/guides/demarches/enedis/recrutement, accessed 01.04.2019). People with disabilities can report to ERDF via a special e-mail address—their CV is then verified by a person specializing in the recruitment of people with disabilities. Many recruitment procedures are also simplified for people with disabilities. ERDF also appears at job fairs. The company also ensures that the situation of the recruitment interview is tailored to the needs of the candidate—for example, the presence of a sign language interpreter can be ensured at the interview. The recruitment process for people with disabilities is more flexible and conducted by consultants dealing with the recruitment of the disabled.

When a disabled employee is hired, the company talks with him or her about adjusting the workplace. During this conversation, information is collected on tools, software and solutions for the organisation of work required by the employee. Adapting the workplace is a challenge for the company due to the long time it takes. The scale of the problem is not large, because only about 10% of persons with disabilities need to adapt the workplace (Kotzian et al. 2014b, p. 259).

Électricité Réseau Distribution France (energy industry, France)—a state enterprise that implements diversity policy, including those addressed to people with disabilities. When concluding contracts with other organisations, it takes into account whether the company employs people with disabilities or has an active CSR policy (Giermanowska 2014c).

When an employee is recruited, the organisations proceed to familiarize the employee with the workplace and work environment. These activities are aimed at preparing a disabled person to perform professional tasks, as well as her co-workers and superiors for better communication and mutual understanding. The confidentiality of information is also important in this process, in line with the expectations of the disabled person. The induction process of employees with disability was based on:

- Preparation and adjustment of the scope of tasks in the organisation to the competencies and health opportunities of employees, often after consultation with a doctor and the disabled person.
- The application of extended time of induction for people with disabilities, often under the care of a job coach.
- Application of various information management procedures dealing with employee's disability when introducing him or her to a new team:
  - making information secret and disclosing it only at the request of a disabled person, especially in a situation of invisible/hidden disability;
  - organizing training for employees with disabilities before the disabled person is accepted for work;
  - informing co-workers of the employee about their health situation, if there was a risk that it could affect their work, contacts with the team or if the vigilance of the team in relation to the worker's health is needed.

An example: Induction of a disabled employee at the European Parliament (Belgium/Luxembourg)

The induction of a disabled employee starts with establishing his/her working time. At the Parliament, employees can work in flexible working time, shortened time, use more frequent breaks or work remotely (teleworking). A high level of adjustment is also characteristic of the work environment. Buildings and offices are adapted to the needs of people on wheelchairs and the visually impaired; in addition, people with disabilities also have necessary technical equipment at their workstations, enabling them to perform their duties efficiently (All new projects for the expansion, renovation or equipment of buildings must fully ensure accessibility for people with disabilities, http://www.europarl.europa.eu/news/pl/faq/23/dostepnosc-parlamentu-europejskiego-dla-osob-niepelnosprawnych, accessed 1.04.2019). There is also an information campaign directed at employees of institutions who are to cooperate with a disabled person. One-day training sessions for a team which is being joined by a disabled person are carried out at the request of the person's superior and cover the following issues:

- knowledge about disability—definition, perception, ways of obtaining information about disability,
- disability policy, procedures and legislation,
- medical and social approach to disability,
- good practices and adjusting the workplace,
- and particularly important: the principles of etiquette in contact with people with disabilities—the way of communication, disability issues.

In the European Parliament, there are also periodic trainings that raise employees' awareness in the area of diversity—gender, nationality and disability (Kotzian et al. 2014b, pp. 290–291). Usually, the induction of the employee runs smoothly, and colleagues warmly welcome a new person into the team, and in case of difficulties—help. The team plays a large role in the process of the induction of every employee, especially a disabled person: that is engagement of the supervisor and other team members. At the Parliament, efforts are being made to eliminate all barriers faced by people with disabilities, but employees are aware that there are still some technical barriers making work of their disabled persons difficult (Kotzian et al. 2014b, p. 291).

European Parliament (public sector, Belgium/Luxembourg)—an international institution that conducts activities promoting solidarity, diversity and equal employment opportunities that are implemented in HR policy In its activities, it refers to many policies and practices in the field of policy of diversity and management of disability issues (Giermanowska 2014c). Parliament offers paid internships for people with disabilities (both university graduates and people without higher education may participate). The programme includes five-month paid internships for people with disabilities and is carried out at the Secretariat of the European Parliament (http://www.eurodesk.pl/granty/praktyki-w-parlamencie-europejskim-dla-osob-niepelnosprawnych, accessed 1.04.2019).

An example: Adaptive training at Dr Irena Eris Cosmetics Laboratory (Poland)

Every employee after the admission to work undergoes an adaptation training lasting from 1 to 7 days. During the training, the employees are familiarized with the health and safety rules, internal regulations, procedures and policies in force in the company. They also need to sign a document certifying their knowledge of corporate values. During the training, non-disabled employees are informed about the possibility of cooperation with disabled people—this element of the programme was introduced by the HR director many years ago, so that employees would not be surprised by the presence of disabled workers and could avoid awkward situations. When a person with a disability is admitted to work, it is necessary to provide the team with additional information, especially when the disability is visible or can affect the work of the team or communication. In addition to the standard information about a new employee, employees are alerted about possible difficulties resulting from the disability of a new employee (e.g. in the case of deaf people) (Kotzian et al. 2014a, p. 165).

The presence of people with disabilities among crew members contributed to the formation of an organisational culture focused on caring for people. In the past, the Laboratory was a sheltered workshop, and today 10% of its employees are people with various disabilities. "*Employing people with disabilities allows us to look from a different perspective, treat certain issues differently, arouse sensitivity* – explains Izabela Chojnacka-Naskręt. - - *It's easier for us to see that productivity does not depend on the number of hours spent at work, but on the involvement of people.*" (Out of concern for people—Laboratorium Kosmetyczne Dr. Irena Eris, no date, *Z troski o człowieka—Laboratorium Kosmetyczne Dr. Irena Eris*, accessed 27.03.2019).

Dr. Irena Eris Cosmetics Laboratory (cosmetics industry, Poland)—the company was established in 1983 as a small crafts-based workshop, employing one employee and producing one type of cream. In 30 years, the company has developed, also gaining foreign markets. Currently, it produces about 20 million cosmetics annually, offers several hundred products and employs nearly one thousand employees. However, its approach to people has been unchanged for years, it is a concern for people. The presence of disabled people is a natural element of the company's organisational culture and the implementation of the idea of socially responsible business (Giermanowska 2014c; *Z troski o człowieka—Laboratorium Kosmetyczne Dr. Irena Eris*, no date, https://rodzinaipraca.gov.pl/dla-pracodawcy/dobre-praktyki/z-troski-o-czlowieka-laboratorium-kosmetyczne-dr-irena-eris/, accessed 27.03.2019).

An example: Employment in accordance with qualifications in the Municipal Public Library in Katowice (Poland)

The assumption of the personnel policy of the Municipal Public Library in Katowice, from the moment when the first disabled employees appeared in the facility, was to employ them as specialists, requiring high qualifications and education. As a result, they are not perceived by co-workers and superiors through the prism of their disability, but through the prism of competence. The consequence of this approach is equal treatment of all employees, understood not only as a lack of discrimination, but also as management of disabled people at work without being lenient towards them. Employees who have proven their competence are entrusted with additional tasks without fear that they will not be able to cope. They also have the opportunity to come up with their own initiative, submit their ideas and implement them (Kotzian et al. 2014a, p. 198).

The library in 2016 employed 187 people, including 13 with various types of disabilities (including: 3 people with a significant degree of disability, 6 people with moderate disability, 4 people with a slight degree of disability) (Report of the Municipal Public Library in Katowice for 2016 (*Sprawozdanie Miejskiej Biblioteki Publicznej w Katowicach za rok 2016*, p. 32)). The library achieved an excellent combination of the implementation of its statutory goals, which include activities for the benefit of the local community, with employing workers with disabilities. These two areas are mutually driven and constitute a path that public institutions should follow.

Municipal Public Library in Katowice (public sector, Poland)—a local government cultural institution in which disabled employees are employed on substantive positions consistent with their qualifications. The library has a tradition of working for the benefit of the community of people with disabilities, which results from its statutory goals. It conducts free activities through 35 branches in all districts of the city, visited mainly by members of the local community, and it strives to meet the needs of various user groups, establishes and consolidates contacts, integrates the communities in which it operates (Giermanowska 2014c; Report of the Municipal Public Library in Katowice for 2016, p. 1).

Employers, in order to effectively deal with and manage disability in an organisation, need to know the needs of people with disability and understand their experiences and perception. One of these issues is the confidentiality of information on disability. Disclosing disability to a potential or current employer is a personal and difficult decision that can have far-reaching consequences for both the employer and the employee. On the one hand, disclosure of disability information can provide the employee with appropriate adjustments at the workplace and help the employer respond more effectively to diversity and inclusion initiatives. On the other hand, disclosure may also result in negative consequences for the employee, such as reduced expectations from the supervisor/manager, isolation from colleagues and an increased probability of termination of contract (von Schrader et al. 2014). Research results focusing on identification and a better understanding of the factors influencing the decision to disclose disability indicate the important role of employers, managers and the working environment. This was supported by activities such as promoting positive relations between manager and employee, training in the area of management, knowledge and awareness of disability, promoting a culture based on the principles of diversity and inclusion in the workplace (e.g. by including disability in the organisation's diversity statement; including people with visible disabilities in the company's promotional material; encouraging applicants with disabilities on recruitment materials). Each of these organisational practices can build employees' trust in the organisation and be a decisive factor in the disclosure of disability. An important factor is also the presence of a person with visible disability in the workplace (von Schrader et al. 2014).

> **An example: Disclosing disability and preparing the team to receive a disabled employee at Thales (France)**

Team members are prepared to receive an employee through disability-related training, including issues such as disability definition, legal regulations, integration and communication with employees, employee management, disability policy in Thales, assistance in employee induction, etc. Each time a disabled person is employed, they are introduced to the team, which earlier learns about the new person, workplace adjustments and necessary tips for communicating with a disabled colleague. Detailed arrangements related to the work contract and information on the terms of cooperation are very important for the team. Sometimes, if a new employee agrees, the type of disability and more detailed information can also be revealed to the team. Thales has a code of ethics, and if there is a situation of discrimination, the person who is a witness or victim may anonymously report a violation of the rules to the Ethics Committee, which deals with resolving the reported situation and if necessary takes appropriate remedial measures. The company's broad preparation for the introduction of a disabled person includes both the preparation of the team and the job position, as well as help of a tutor (Kotzian et al. 2014b, p. 252).

Thales Group (arms, aerospace and land transport industry, France)—a French electronics corporation, the company, since the 1990s, has developed practices in the field of employment and management of employees with disabilities. It works with many organisations and disseminates CSR ideas, including those on disability, also internationally (Giermanowska 2014c). Thales offers employment opportunities for disabled people, even in countries where this is not required by law, by cooperating with local committees. A dedicated integration unit, known as Thales Mission Insertion, has been set up in France, supported by Disability Employment Committees in all Thales entities with more than 250 employees (https://www.thalesgroup.com/en/global/corporate-responsibility/employees/equality-and-diversity, accessed 2.04.2019).

3 Adapting the Workplace and Assistantship

Employing a worker with a disability is linked with adaptation of the workplace, working conditions and tasks to the needs of a person with disability. Adapting the workplace is a CRPD requirement and is associated with reasonable accommodation (Article 27 CRPD). Reasonable accommodation is understood as a tool for ensuring equality resulting from individual rights, including the right to work. It means introducing necessary and appropriate replacements or adjustments that do not cause excessive and disproportionate expenses on the part of the employer and enable disabled people to do the work. In other words, as Marianne Hirschberg and Christian Papadopoulos (2016, p. 9) conclude, reasonable accommodation is based on three important rules:

1. the necessity of an accommodation for the disabled person in question in a specific situation,
2. a proportionate burden for the institution (state, employer or similar) providing the accommodation
3. and with the objective of being able to exercise all human rights and fundamental freedoms on an equal basis with others.

In good practices, reasonable accommodation is an important distinctive feature of organisations focusing on diversity. It is contained in a series of activities referred to as adjusting the workplace. In addition, the form, time and place of work are adjusted to the needs of a person with disability. An analysis of good practices indicates that this involves:

- Purchase of the appropriate equipment needed for people with sensory disabilities, e.g. braille displays, speech synthesizers, speaking devices and software adapted for people with disabilities.
- Adaptation of space to the requirements of a disabled person, e.g. appropriate marking of rooms and creation of appropriately wide passes for wheelchairs.
- Adaptation of the communication system in the company, e.g. bypassing paper communication in the presence of people with visual disabilities in the company or simplifying messages in the case of people with intellectual disabilities and offering sign language courses for hearing employees, employing a sign language interpreter.

- Flexibility of the form of employment and working time, e.g. introduction of flexible working time and introduction of remote work at the employee's request.
- Adjusting the location of employment in the event of a permanent workplace with the employer to the needs of workers with disabilities, e.g. in the case of companies with branches, employment of employees in the branches closest to their place of residence.
- Provision of transport to the workplace.
- Providing personal assistance services (and paying it).

An example: Adjusting the work environment in the Office of the Ombudsman (Poland)

The management of the Office strives to ensure that people with disabilities do not encounter any barriers in accessing information on the Office's activities and employment opportunities it offers as well as at the employment stage. The building has architectural barriers, but it is accessible to people using a wheelchair. The website has the appropriate font, colours and contrast that make it accessible to the visually impaired. To meet the needs and expectations of deaf people (https://www.rpo.gov.pl/, accessed 30.03.2019).

The office organized a sign language course for its employees. Its idea is to facilitate the communication of employees of the Office with people with hearing impairments in order to efficiently handle such clients and to remove communication barriers with deaf colleagues. One of the people with a significant degree of disability was employed as part of the competition for the position of a legal clerk. This workstation has been adapted to the specific needs of a person moving on a wheelchair—a separate room was organized on the ground floor of the building with easy access to the toilet, and necessary computer equipment was purchased (scanner, special mouse pad). Adjustment of the position took place thanks to funding from PFRON (State Fund for the Rehabilitation of the Disabled made up of employers' contributions not employing the required amount of disabled people). However, it was not possible to obtain funds to ensure the daily travel to work of this person. However, the office has been flexible in the way the disabled person's working time is organized, and part of the time he works from home. Due to a significant degree of disability, this employee also benefits from the support of a personal assistant paid by the Office (Kotzian et al. 2014a, p. 203).

Office of the Ombudsman (public sector, Poland)—a public institution in which the employment of disabled people is consistent with the public role of the Ombudsman, initiatives taken by him and internal documents of the Office. In 2011, the Committee of Experts on Persons with Disabilities was established, which supports the Ombudsman in the implementation of his statutory tasks in the field of monitoring the freedoms and rights of persons with disabilities (Giermanowska 2014c; https://www.rpo.gov.pl/pl/content/meeting-commission-experts-persons-with-disabilities-13-02-18, accessed 30.03.2019).

An example: Employment of people with intellectual disabilities in a restaurant chain Max Hamburgerrestauranger (Sweden)

The company focuses its activities on people with intellectual disabilities, and the process of their recruitment has several different elements. One of them is reporting the demand for an employee to Samhall (an organisation using public funds, acting for the professional activation of disabled people), which deals with the search for the right people. The second element is the process of checking the candidate's suitability for the position. After about 8 weeks of the trial period, the company already knows if the employee can perform his duties and continue working in the company—sometimes that the scope of the employee's responsibilities changes after this period. The process of adjusting the scope of duties is so accurate due to the group of employees—the company focuses on employing people with intellectual disabilities. From the Max's point of view, the advantage of candidates with this kind of disability is that they do not have any physical barriers that would make it difficult to perform the duties related to maintaining the restaurant. Furthermore, in the case of people with intellectual disabilities, it is also not necessary to adapt work posts or equip them with additional equipment.

The programme of employing people with disabilities in Max can be assessed positively, although it is not without problems. The company has set itself the goal of employing at least two people with disabilities in each facility. Access to the programme by individual restaurants takes place on a voluntary basis. Thanks to this, people with disabilities do not face dislike from managers and regular employees. On the other hand, this voluntariness somewhat inhibits the development of the programme. The biggest problem is prejudice, especially among managers who perceive disabled employees as unable to perform certain professional tasks. Hence, the company attaches great importance to the education of managers in matters related to disability and prejudice (Kotzian et al. 2014b, p. 268).

Max Hamburgerrestauranger (restaurant industry, Sweden)—the largest chain of fast food restaurants in Sweden. An organisation with an extensive programme of employment of disabled people, including those with intellectual disabilities. Employment of disabled people is included in its diversity and sustainable development policies (Giermanowska 2014c). Currently, the company has 120 restaurants around the world and employs approximately 5400 employees worldwide (https://www.maxburgers.com/Home/about-max/About-Max/, accessed 2.04.2019).

An example: Adjustment of workstations and organisation of working time in the IT company Altix (Poland)

Because the Altix board of directors includes people with disabilities, any barriers or difficulties that such people encounter in other places are immediately noticed and removed here. The company provides employees with all the equipment they need—Braille displays, speech synthesizers and speaking devices. The chairman of the company believes that despite the costs incurred in this respect, employing disabled people pays off. Almost all Altix employees are employed under a contract of employment. The company is characterized by great flexibility in the approach to work organisation—you can work in a flexible working time or in the teleworking system. Visually impaired people can count on the help of co-workers or the company's support in performing activities that are difficult for them (e.g. a company of a colleague without visual impairment and assistance with travel during business trips). The position of the company regarding employment and adjusting the workplace to the needs of disabled employees is noteworthy. Blind people are employed in almost all positions except for those whose performance would be significantly impeded or impossible due to the type of disability (e.g. work in the secretariat, warehouse or service). Most disabled people work in IT positions. The blind and visually impaired are also traders and telemarketers at Altix (Kotzian et al. 2014a, p. 122).

The internal IT system used by the company, especially in the aspect of communication and project management, helps to run things smoothly. This system records working time, allows sending notes and messages and sets up discussion groups on selected topics. It is also used to assign tasks to employees. It is used by all employees, regardless of whether they are disabled or not (Kotzian et al. 2014a, p. 123).

Altix (IT industry, Poland)—an organisation that conducts extensive CSR activities and engages employees in actions for people with disabilities. It established the "Szansa dla Niewidomych" (Opportunity for the Blind) Foundation and promotes employee volunteering (Giermanowska 2014c). The company actively supports and promotes the employment of people with disabilities. In 28/03/2019, it took part in the conference "Innovations in employing people with disabilities" at the University of Economics in Poznań, where it presented the application: Your Way—created by Altix and MobiAsystent for the Foundation "Szansa dla Niewidomych" (Opportunity for the Blind). It also presented equipment that improves the work and everyday life of the blind and visually impaired (http://www.altix.pl/pl/aktualnosci/konferencja-innowacje-w-zatrudnianiu-osob-niepelnosprawnych-w-pozniniu/, accessed 30.03.2019).

4 Keeping the Employee in Employment and Employee Development

Retaining an employee with a disability in employment requires not only proper preparation of the position along with adjusting the time, form and place of work. Increasingly companies realize that they should develop health and rehabilitation programmes in the workplace, supporting and increasing workers' work ability. The concept of work ability since the 1990s has been developed and disseminated by scientists from the Finnish Institute of Occupational Health. It means searching for a balance between the employee's abilities (resulting from his/her health, functional abilities, competence and skills) and the requirements of the job position (Ilmarinen 2009, p. 2). It emphasizes the dynamics of mutual adjustment of human capabilities and work requirements, which forces constant monitoring of the skills, health and condition of the staff (Ilmarinen 2009). For this purpose, the Work Ability Index (WAI) was developed. It is the sum of 7 elements: two objectives (number of diseases diagnosed by a doctor and sick leave in the last year) and five parameters describing individual job performance abilities (Ilmarinen 2007).

WAI can be used by organisations applying age and/or disability management in their personnel strategies. "The maintenance and promotion of work ability requires good cooperation between supervisors and employees. However, neither can ensure that work ability will not change; instead, the responsibility is shared between the employer and the employee. Work ability is not, however, only a matter of these two. The management and human resource policy of the enterprise sets the framework for the promotion of work ability, and the work community can also play an important role in supporting the work ability of its members. Central roles are also played by the occupational health care and occupational safety organization" (Ilmarinen 2009, p. 2).

The conclusions drawn from the WAI score obtained can be a valuable indication for the occupational physician and HR departments about the directions of further action towards employees. At the organisational level, the use of the WAI indicator enables both interventions (in terms of improving working conditions, health care of employees), as well as promotional campaigns in the area of promoting a healthy lifestyle through health education (Malińska 2017, p. 20). This is in line with EU guidelines regarding the role of physicians supervising employees who should be advisers to the employee and the entire organisation, agents of changes in the workplace (detection and indication of organisational irregularities, suggesting changes, methods and means of their implementation), information system coordinators (gathering, dissemination of information related to health and safety in the work process, design and implementation of training programmes and promoting health) (Bugajska et al. 2010, p. 61).

The review of good practices related to employing people with disabilities indicated that organisations caring for retaining an employee in employment were aware of the necessary activities in the field of health promotion and invested in the health of employees and the safety of their work by:

- The development of rehabilitation services at the workplace, which allows the employee to return to work in the event of a disability being acquired during the employment period, cooperation in the field of rehabilitation with health-care facilities.
- Implementation of the procedure of monitoring the health of employees in the event of prolonged periods of absence at work.
- Retraining the employee, transferring the employee to other positions corresponding to his current state of health and fitness, adjusted according to the guidelines of the occupational medicine doctor.
- Financing or subsidizing the costs of private health insurance for employees.
- Offering health services to employees purchased from the organisation's partner.

An example: Employee vocational rehabilitation programme at the Ford-Werke GmbH automotive company (Germany)

The company undertakes adaptation measures for every employee whose sick leave is 30 days or more. This is due to legal provisions in Germany and is aimed at preventing further abstention of the employee. The vocational rehabilitation programme starts with the employee's examinations carried out by the company doctor, who determines further conditions of his employment and indicates the necessary adaptations to work. Next, the existing work environment is evaluated and the necessary adjustments are made in the working conditions or in the form of work performance. The next stage is the gradual induction of the employee to new responsibilities. At the same time, the employee is subject to occupational rehabilitation, partially paid for from the company's health insurance. Rehabilitation at the workplace is also offered. In the rehabilitation process, the company cooperates with health-care entities, rehabilitation centres and other organisations. The entire process of restoring an employee to work is subject to a final evaluation along with a satisfaction survey (Kotzian et al. 2014b, p. 229).

Ford-Werke GmbH (automotive company, Germany)—branch of the American Ford Motor Company, a company that promotes diversity and sustainable development policies in all its branches.

It develops employee volunteering programmes. The company's activities in the field of disability are based on many documents of state and international law and internal company regulations (Giermanowska 2014c). Ford-Werke (Germany) was honoured several times for their outstanding diversity programme. The company has an individual ability-oriented approach. Responsibility is transferred to operational managers, with the support of the Disability Management Team. Priority in all measures is given to the individuality of the Ford employees and their right to self-determination (https://www.enwhp.org/resources/toolip/doc/2018/04/20/ph_work_disability_management_ford_germany.pdf, accessed 1.04.2019).

The development of pro-health programmes for employees and maintaining good working conditions for employees is becoming an important element of HRM strategy. The number of organisations appreciating the importance of well-being programmes is increasing, e.g. in 2018 Poland, they were considered to be an important HR trend and a very good business investment (Ułamek et al. 2019, p. 10). Their goal is to care for the well-being (physical, psychological and social) of employees, to attract and retain them in the company in times of decreasing and ageing workforce. Although the health and working conditions of employees in EU countries improve systematically, the significance of the risk of cancer caused by the place and character of work and the deteriorating mental health of employees is still pointed out. EU countries are aware of the costs of sick leave and employee absences for both organisations and employees. The basic component of well-being programmes is providing medical care for employees, implementing preventive programmes and caring for the mental condition of employees, taking into account their diversity due to age, nature of work and family development phase (Ułamek et al. 2019). Well-being programmes are also of great benefit for employees with disabilities.

Organisations paid a lot of attention to the development of their employees. Employers stressed that disabled employees should have opportunities for career development and promotion at the workplace. Organisations should create equal opportunities for all employees in acquiring the skills and professional experience necessary for their further professional career. These goals were achieved through the following practices:

- Organizing training for employees in the workplace or outside the workplace, guaranteeing the necessary adjustments.
- Co-financing of trainings by the employer and from other funds allocated for improving the qualifications of disabled employees.
- Availability of information about training and vacancies at the workplace.
- Encouraging disabled employees to raise their professional qualifications and standing.
- Evaluating the performance of disabled employees according to the same criteria as those applied to employees performing the same or similar work.
- Supervising the management process of a disabled employee by HR departments.

An example: Division of tasks, evaluation, access to training and promotion in the automotive company Hutchinson (Poland)

In Hutchinson, the disability itself does not affect the area and position of employment either in the administrative departments or on the production line. In production departments, people with disabilities have an additional ten minutes break, but during this time they are replaced by their colleagues. Another standard of work was only introduced for those who are wheelchair bound, when the doctor recommended appropriate modifications. A very similar employee appraisal system applies. The mobility index on the production line is slightly different. Able-bodied employees are assessed for the actual ability of servicing many jobs, and disabled employees for being prepared to acquire such skills in a situation where the company adjusts the relevant workstations. Access to training and promotion is not diversified according to the employee's disability. When recruiting, the potential of the employee is taken into account, which makes it possible to create a suitable career path for him (Kotzian et al. 2014a, pp. 154–156).

Hutchinson (automotive industry, Poland)—an international company belonging to the Total Group—a leader in the automotive, aerospace and consumer products industry. An enterprise in which the employment of disabled people is inscribed in the CSR, and the principle of diversity and non-discrimination are included in the company's value system and that of the Total Group to which the company belongs (Giermanowska 2014c). The company in its branches in Poland constantly encourages people with disabilities to take up employment, emphasizing this in job advertisements: "We also encourage people with disabilities to apply. For us, work and disability are not mutually exclusive" (https://www.placpigal.pl/praca_dla_osob_z_orzeczeniem_o_stopniu_niepelnosprawnosci,20170623073358.html, accessed 30.03.2019).

An example: Setting goals, tasks and employee development at the cosmetics company Marionnaud Parfumeries (France)

Following employment, disabled employee undergoes standard training regarding the company and work at Marionnaud (three-day integration training), and position-based instruction. In the initial period of employment, a person with disability, may perform their tasks with the help of a job coach, who has experience in supporting employees with a specific type of disability. Before an employee starts work, working hours and the scope of the employee's duties are consulted and agreed with the doctor. Job induction process is standardized, mainly due to the type of disability of employed persons and difficulties caused by it. Workers with disabilities are warmly welcomed and looked after by the team The presence of a worker with disabilities has a positive impact on the atmosphere at work and relations within a team (Kotzian et al. 2014b, p. 244).

Disability is taken into account when setting goals and evaluating employees, but generally, these processes are similar to those of able-bodied employees. Greater understanding applies only to situations that are associated with difficulties in performing tasks that result from disability. In Marionnaud, there are also no obstacles for disabled people to take part in training or to be promoted—each time, however, the doctor decides whether there are no medical contraindications.

The anti-discrimination policy of the company emphasizes the attitude towards the disabled, because the company's goal is to employ as many of them as possible. If an employee feels that his or her rights have been violated, he or she may contact the HR department. In case of newly employed employees, especially those with disabilities, their satisfaction and induction process are monitored by the HR department, which personally contacts each employee (Kotzian et al. 2014b, p. 245).

Marionnaud Parfumeries (cosmetics industry, France)—French perfumery chain, manufactures and distributes perfumes, cosmetics and beauty products in France and internationally. An organisation undertaking activities in the field of corporate social responsibility addressed to the disabled, it cooperates with organisations associating the disabled and government organisations (Giermanowska 2014c, https://www.marionnaud.fr/, accessed 2.04.2019).

An example: Managing disabled employees at the Main Inspectorate of Plant Health and Seed Inspection (PIORIN), Central Laboratory—Toruń (Poland)

A disability of an employee is treated as one of his characteristics, analogous to personality traits or the type of skills possessed. It is taken into account when assigning tasks. All employees are accountable for tasks performed and goals achieved. Employees with disabilities have the same access to training and promotions as their able-bodied colleagues. At the Inspectorate, team diversity is given high priority, and a lot of attention is given to appropriate communication within individual teams and between members of various teams. This is facilitated by family like organisational culture (the entity employs a small number of people) and individual approach to employees (Kotzian et al. 2014a, pp. 212–213).

Main Inspectorate of Plant Health and Seed Inspection, Central Laboratory (public sector, Poland)—an institution, conducting a policy of making employees aware of their rights and possibilities resulting from the status of a disabled employee. It cares for employees who acquired disability during employment (Giermanowska 2014c).

---

5 Disability Management in the Workplace

Disability management in the workplace should be an integral part of the human resources development strategy in the organisation. This strategy should be consulted with representatives of the employees of the organisation, including disabled employees and their representatives.

Employee participation, understood as the participation of persons with disabilities in managing their affairs in the workplace, is of key importance for the integration process, increasing employment and retaining disabled persons in the organisation. These issues are raised in the previously mentioned documents such as: "ILO code of practice: Managing disability in the workplace" (2002) or "Code of Good Practice for the Employment of People with Disabilities" adopted by the Bureau of the European Parliament (2005). It should be emphasized that in the organisations surveyed by us, most did not have a separate strategy concerning only people with disabilities. Disability management in the workplace was, however, an important element of the human resources development strategy and included issues such as equal opportunities policy and non-discrimination, and sometimes diversity management policy.

Good practices in managing disability issues in the workplace have taken various forms in the organisations under study:

- Organisations that have taken appropriate action on personnel procedures have emphasized the key role of cooperation and communication with organisations representing employees and with employees, including people with disabilities, in developing and adopting those solutions.
- Efforts were made to ensure comprehensive and coherent actions in the field of internal policy related to the management of disability issues, with activities outside the organisation (e.g. CSR).
- Organisations used various forms of increasing the level of awareness of all employees and managers in the field of disability issues, e.g. through trainings, workshops and internal communications addressed to employees of the organisation.
- In terms of information exchange and training, the knowledge of other specialized institutions or expert groups dealing with disability issues was used.
- Employers sometimes sought to disseminate information about good practices related to the employment of disabled people among other employers, their contractors and the local environment.
- In some organisations, research was conducted to assess the effectiveness of policies for disabled people; the results were published and errors were corrected.

> **An example: Managing a diverse team at the restaurant company Allehånde Køkken (Denmark)**

According to supervisors, managing a diverse team, in which the proportions between able-bodied and disabled employees are equal, has its specificity. These people need to learn to work together, and it takes time to know each other and integrate. Able-bodied and disabled employees are treated the same—but the differences between them are the subject of discussion in the company. None of the groups is discriminated against or treated specifically, but that does not mean that there are no differences. As in any team, there are difficult moments among Allehånde employees—there will always be frustrations when different people are together. Equal treatment at Allehånde applies to all processes in the company. Both setting goals and accounting for their implementation. The company, operating on the open market, must achieve its goals and employees must perform their tasks. Everyone is held accountable for the results and how they are achieved using the same criteria (Kotzian et al. 2014b, p. 122).

Allehånde Køkken (restaurant industry, Denmark)—a socially responsible company that employs people with disabilities and works for the benefit of the disabled. The mission of the organisation is professional activation of disabled people in connection with the implementation of business goals (Giermanowska 2014c). The company employs and trains deaf people to become professional cooks. Four times in recent years they have won prizes based on the project of education and employment of young deaf people (http://www.allehaande.dk/om-os, accessed 02.04.2019).

> **An example: Diversity policy in a company providing comprehensive commercial real estate services Sodexo (Poland)**

The programme of employing disabled people run by Sodexo Poland is a model for company branches located in other countries. At the company, good preparation for employing disabled people, including training in Poland and abroad, an information campaign addressed to both regular employees and managers, using various types of support programmes, e.g. *Leonardo da Vinci programme* and cooperation with various non-governmental organisations draws attention.

The company emphasizes its commitment to the principle of respect for diversity on its websites: "The people that we employ are of the greatest value to us, as a company, which is why we strive to make the workplace friendly, open to diversity and diversity, because only thanks to this we can continue to develop and be successful" (https://pl.sodexo.com/home/kariera/dlaczego-sodexo/roznorodnosc-i-integracja.html, accessed 1.04.2019).

A very broad understanding of the concept of diversity in a company that creates teams diverse in terms of gender, age and disability is noteworthy. It is worth emphasizing that employing people with intellectual dysfunctions is an extremely rare phenomenon on the open labour market in Poland. Meanwhile, people with disabilities, visually impaired and intellectually disabled work side by side in Sodexo, supporting and helping each other. This has a positive impact not only on the effects of work, but also on employee morale. The disabled are indeed part of the team—they take part in team building meetings, have their circle of friends and are treated as equals at work. Equal treatment is possible, because the company attaches great importance to the proper fit of the person to the position. Sodexo employs disabled people, using the help of non-governmental organisations. The company managers pay attention to the level of readiness of these organisations for cooperation with enterprises, the need to have access to current database of candidates for work, which would on the one hand increase their employability, on the other hand, it would allow the employer to quickly fill the vacancy (Kotzian et al. 2014a, p. 189).

Sodexo (commercial real estate service, Poland)—an international company that provides comprehensive services for real estate: catering, building administration, technical services and cleaning. It implements a global policy of equal opportunities, opposing exclusion and discrimination and implementing measures for corporate social responsibility. The company is committed to creating a work environment that is friendly to people with disabilities. In Poland, disabled people are mainly employed in units providing food-related services. It cooperates with many organisations supporting the employment of disabled people and job centres. It promotes the employment of disabled people, including by informing in job advertisements about a work environment friendly to disabled people (Giermanowska 2014c, https://pl.sodexo.com/home/kariera/ddlaczego-sodexo/roznorodnosc-i-integration.html, accessed 1.04.2019).

An example: Rehab Station Stockholm—disabled people are in our team

Rehab Station employs disabled employees at key positions for the organisation. Their role in the company is huge—they share knowledge about the problems of disabled people with their colleagues, promote the organisation through participation in sporting events, including Paralympics, and above all establish perfect contact with the patient and constitute for him a vivid example of social and professional activity (Kotzian et al. 2014b, p. 278).

The employment of workers with disabilities at the company was also fostered by the owner of Rehab, who is himself disabled, and understands perfectly the problems of other people with disfunctions and does not think about them in terms of barriers and limitations, but people whom he can employ. The state policy, which provides the company and its employees with significant financial support, also facilitates the employment of workers with disability. The presence of disabled people in the company is something natural. The company is aware of the benefits brought by employing people with disabilities. The coherence of its activities is noteworthy: the company deals with the comprehensive rehabilitation of disabled people, and its CSR activities are fully consistent with its tasks. Rehab Station finances research, helps in rehabilitation, sometimes conducts training for companies, sponsors sports events and sportsmen and employs people with disabilities. In addition, the company encourages other companies to hire people with disabilities (Kotzian et al. 2014b, p. 279).

Rehab Station Stockholm (rehabilitation branch, Sweden)—a company that develops and conducts rehabilitation and personal assistance on a national and international scale. The organisation applies the approach of rehabilitation of disabled people by disabled people. The owner, who is himself disabled, and state policy offering significant financial support to the company and its employees favour the employment of people with disabilities (Giermanowska 2014a, http://www.rehabstation.se/ Rehabilitering/Om-oss/Organisation/, accessed 2.04. 2019).

6 Employer's Image and Disability

Enterprises applying good practices, as demonstrated by analyses in the area of diversity management, are usually aware of the importance of the company's image and reputation in business operations (*The Business Case for Diversity: Good Practices in the Workplace* 2005, p. 25). In communicating with the external and internal environment, organisations try to convey the principles and values that guide them. They also develop partnerships and contacts with organisations from public sectors (including universities) and non-public ones. They try for prizes, apply for competitions related to HR initiatives, take part in charity events or support local traditions. Their visibility is relatively high, also at industry conferences or in the wide range of business.

In good practices of employing people with disabilities, analysed by us, developing the image of the employer was a conscious strategy of the organisation that actively participated in the life of local communities and in the business world. Their actions were distinguished by:

- Using the fact of employing disabled people as part of the communication strategy at the global level (in the case of companies with many international branches) as well as at the local level (e.g. using appropriate formulas in recruitment advertisements); however, some companies avoid using the image of disabled employees due to the industry or sector in which they operate (e.g. insurance companies or high-ranking public organisations).
- Participation in competitions designed for employers developing their personnel policies.
- Participation in industry conferences and communication of their mission, conducting training for employers regarding the employment of disabled people.
- Participation in conferences for people with disabilities.
- Running or participating in meetings aimed at increasing the social awareness of the external environment, e.g. students of local universities.
- Establishment of own non-governmental organisations that deal with activities supporting vocational activation of disabled people, financing scholarships for vocational education and training for people with disabilities, sponsoring activities corresponding to the company's profile of activities related to disability.

- Building employees' social awareness through internal communication, e.g. placing information on employee rights on the intranet or conducting actions and training and regular employee satisfaction survey.
- Creating and disseminating catalogues of good practices, brochures on CSR activities or referring to business ethics.
- Transparency of employment information, including matters related to people with disabilities.

An example: Carrefour Poland—a company that encourages other employers

Carrefour shares information that it employs people with disabilities, but the goal of the organisation in its communication activities is not so much to build the image, but rather to encourage other companies to take similar practices. The Carrefour Group states that in 2015, 11.2 thousand workers with disabilities worked for them. In the Polish branch of the French company, about 800 people with disabilities worked at the time—as part of direct and indirect employment, which was about 7% of the entire crew. (https://www.wiadomoscihandlowe.pl/artykuly/carrefour-zatrudnia-ponad-11-tys-osobniepelnospra,9933, accessed 1.04.2019).

EKON association (a social enterprise and the Platform for the Integration of Disabled Persons PION operating within its framework, engaged in professional activation of disabled people) take care, on behalf of Carrefour Poland, of communication with potential workers. Carrefour prides itself on employing people with disabilities in internal communication directed to employees. This communication is also supposed to build their social awareness. The effects are visible. In the Carrefour employee engagement study, diversity was among the top three rated by employees (May 2011). According to the human resources director, employing disabled people is associated on the one hand with economic benefits for employers and on the other with social benefits. Thanks to working with people with disabilities, the awareness of employees changes as well (Kotzian et al. 2014a, p. 135).

Carrefour Polska (commercial network, Poland)—the policy of sustainable development in the area of CSR is implemented by an international trade network in three areas: economy, environmental protection and society. In Poland, the company established cooperation with the Polski Związek Głuchych (Polish Deaf Association), Niepełnosprawni dla Środowiska EKON (the Disabled for the Environment EKON) association and the Platforma Integracji Osób Niepełnosprawnych PION (Platform of Integration of People with Disabilities). Carrefour was the first retail chains in Poland to sign, in 2013, the International Diversity Charter, thus confirming its commitment to spreading the idea of equality, intergenerational dialogue and professional activation of disabled people (Giermanowska 2014c; https://pszk.pl/profil/carrefour, accessed 1.04.2019).

An example: IKEA Deutschland—organisation open to all social groups

IKEA around the world, in all its locations, attaches great importance to building the image of an entrepreneur who is guided by clear rules. IKEA stores are adapted to the needs of families and the disabled, and the company promotes pro-ecological behaviour, conducts extensive CSR activities. The company also takes care of its image as an employer. It participates in many rankings and competitions, clearly communicates its values to attract people who share them and speaks on its website with the voice of employees. In PR communication, however, it emphasizes diversity in general and not employing disabled people in particular, which it does not boast about publicly either.

IKEA is aware, however, that employing people with dysfunctions positively affects its image, both inside and outside the organisation. On the one hand, employees have a sense of stability and employment security. On the other hand, the company has problems in Germany with finding specialist and management staff, which is why it looks after its image and makes en effort to be perceived as an attractive employer. IKEA is an employer that is open to all—not only people with disabilities, but also other social groups (Kotzian et al. 2014b, pp. 239–240).

IKEA Deutschland (retail trade industry, Germany)—an organisation that is part of the Swedish IKEA network. The company applies high standards of people management, promoting egalitarianism, openness and diversity. It attaches great importance to ecology and pro-social activities in the field of CSR (Giermanowska 2014c, https://seeacareerwithus.com/about-us/our-values, accessed 2.04.2019).

> **An example: We have to set an example—the Department of Social Integration of Disabled People in Cyprus**

The Department of Social Integration of the Disabled People employs people with disabilities in their own team. It conducts business based on the knowledge and experience of disabled employees. Thanks to this, it implements solutions better adapted to the needs of people with disabilities. Employment of people with disabilities is a manifestation of the subjective treatment of beneficiaries and genuine willingness to include them in social life.

The Department is trying to publicize its activities. Every year, it publishes a report on the employment of disabled people, to encourage employers to employ such employees. It mainly conducts information activities using modern forms of communication (Kotzian et al. 2014b, pp. 286–287).

The Department of Social Integration of Disabled People (public sector, Cyprus)—a public institution, its statutory tasks include supporting people with disabilities in the field of social and vocational rehabilitation. In developing activities for people with dysfunctions, the organisation uses the knowledge and experience of employees with disabilities working at the department (Giermanowska 2014c). The Department's website contains continuous and direct information about the main responsibilities and activities of the Department, the legislation that is being promoted and implemented, as well as about the provided services to the citizens (http://www.mlsi.gov.cy/mlsi/dsid/dsid.nsf/dsipd01_en/dsipd01_en?OpenDocum, accessed 2.04.2019).

> **An example: Focusing on the employee, Rudek—a company dealing with medical rehabilitation (Poland)**

A positive aspect of the recruitment process at Rudek, a company providing rehabilitation services, lies in the meeting with a disabled person (the company's owner) and the candidate at the level of recruitment, which on the one hand is part of the process verifying the candidate's competences, and on the other hand, it is the first stage of becoming a part of a diverse organisation, employing both able-bodied and disabled employees. A good side of the recruitment process is also the fact that the candidate's competences are decisive in getting employed (although the company could desire to employ a disabled candidate simply to obtain financial support from PFRON). An important advantage of the company's practices is the proper preparation of the team for the reception of a disabled colleague (information about the help he/she will need from able-bodied colleagues). An open and non-formalized organisational culture, which focuses on individual approach and builds teamwork and flexibility in the division of duties between able-bodied and disabled employees, makes diversity of the team useful in building engagement and a good atmosphere at work and a good relationship with the clients (Kotzian et al. 2014a, p. 179).

The company has huge potential in the form of committed employees ready to participate in promotional campaigns. This potential is appreciated by managers and employees of Rudek—the image of a good employer in the medical industry translates into the perception of the company by customers and thus builds its strong market position (Kotzian et al. 2014a, p. 180).

Rudek—medical rehabilitation clinic (medical rehabilitation, Poland)—an organisation (Non-public health-care facility) that is characterized by a symbiosis between the profile of the company (its clients include people with disabilities) and the employment of disabled workers. The owner of the company is a disabled person himself, and employment of disabled people is an integral element of the company's personnel policy. The company also uses many forms of institutional support offered by PFRON, which allows it to increase employment (Giermanowska 2014c, http://www.rudek.com.pl/o-nas, accessed 1.04.2019).

7 Good Practices Raising Doubts: The Negative Side of Good Practices

The literature on the subject emphasizes the slowness of the diffusion of good practices in business and even within one organisation (Rutkowski 2006, p. 4). The barriers to their dissemination are related to the lack of knowledge among organisations about current good practices, lack of motivation for changes related to their implementation or lack of knowledge and skills among employees of the organisation to implement them. Some researchers are also sceptical about the possibility of disseminating good practices through imitation. It is noted that each organisation has a unique history, organisational culture and operates in a specific place and time. This suggests restrictions on applying good practices, which should rather be treated as "a tool facilitating the search for specific, exemplary solutions in the complex reality, closest to the needs and conditions of an organization" (Brajer-Marczak 2017, p. 17).

Good practices, despite their name, do not always have to be "good" for the organisation that applies them. Business auditors emphasize that despite the presumption of benefits from good practices, they may be detrimental to employees and organisations or counterproductive in achieving a goal set by entrepreneurs (Tran 2016). In principle, good practices are to regulate those areas of activities that are not strictly defined, internally determined or regulated by law. However, good practices are conceptualized and implemented by people who define what is right and what is wrong. Their subjective expectations, situational or cultural-historical context may cause the organisation to distort good practices, applying them in an inflexible way (unadjusted to the place or the occurring social or legal changes). Some dubious good practices may give companies even short-term profits, such as in the case of gifts for contractors, but in the long run such actions may lead to losses as a result of violation of law or image loss (Tran 2016). Louis Grenier (2017) draws attention to similar threats, who using his own example, shows the loses caused by copying good practice of another company in his own affairs. Grenier (2017, no page) warns:

- "What works for another business might not work for yours",
- "Most best practices are past practices",
- "Best practices can harm your business (and even kill it)".

Companies often forget that their organisation is unique and needs tailor-made practices. It is good for the organisation to build its own "bank of internal best practices" (Grenier 2017, no page). Following an authority, whether legal or a market leader, or blindly following the trends of current fashion, organisations implement activities that do not bring them benefits and may even harm employees and business relations.

In the perspective of employment of people with disabilities, the threat may be the instrumental treatment of employment of disabled people as a result of the forced practice of applying the principle of diversity management. The fight for human rights and supporting various discriminated minorities have forced organisations to introduce practices related to diversity management into the policy of managing human resources. However, as Agnieszka Kołodziej-Durnaś emphasizes, diversity management can be not only a form of inclusion, organisational innovation, but it can also lead to "instrumentalization, ideologization or manipulation of identity" and be a far cry from fashionable slogans of: "Participation in management, empowerment of employees and discriminated groups" (Kołodziej-Durnaś 2011, p. 501). In this perspective, the employed employee with disability is the "mascot of inclusion, her privileged status seems to carry the message: being similar to normals [i.e. people without disabilities – note from the author], even at the level of behaviour, is ennobling" (Zakrzewska-Manterys 2008, p. 342). Meanwhile, it is not about the imitation of the behaviour of able-bodied people by disabled individuals or about the manifestation of fashionable ideas or ideologies at the organisational level, but about dignifying work, at a position of substance for which one has necessary qualification, performed by a person, whose disability is but one of his many characteristics.

In the analysis of good practices, the task of a sociologist is to expose the hidden functions and dysfunctions that are unintentional consequences of the phenomenon, discovering real rather than apparent activities and hidden intentions pursued under the slogan of postulates for equality and justice (Kołodziej-Durnaś 2011, p. 502). These problems are well illustrated by the case below describing the employment of a visually impaired person in a large international corporation.

Case study: Cornelia and her struggles with good practices

Cornelia worked for several years in an international outsourcing corporation, in one of the largest cities in Poland. She was employed as part of a CSR project implemented in partnership with a non-governmental organisation, the aim of which was to adapt existing jobs for people with disabilities. Initially, the focus was on adaptations for visually impaired people (blind and visually impaired). The company prides itself on the fact that it does not create special jobs for people with disabilities, it only adapts existing jobs, without using the PFRON subsidy.

Cornelia is a blind university graduate, who speaks several foreign languages. Her workstation has been equipped with a computer with a screen reading programme and speech synthesis.

Initially, the workplace seemed attractive and conducive to development: work in an international environment, the ability to use foreign languages, emphasis on employee development and an extensive system of benefits for employees. Importantly, employees from the Cornelia team were trained in disability awareness. In the first months of her work, she received support in the field of spatial orientation in the workplace and assistance during the induction process.

However, after a few years, Cornelia decided to leave her job, not seeing any opportunities for development and promotion.

What failed to work?

The first mistake was the inclusion of the process of hiring employees with disabilities in the company to the CSR department. There was a lack in the organisational structure of a person whose task would be to support employees with disabilities. Cornelia: "*Whenever I encountered any difficulties related to, for example, work, resulting from the unavailability of the software, I was referred to the CSR manager, who could not do anything about it*".

There was a lack of disability and accessibility management strategy at the workplace. When implementing the project, it was assumed that making one-time adaptations in the form of purchase of assistive technologies is enough for an employee with disability to perform his duties on an equal footing with others, and develop, train, and consequently, advance. There was no monitoring of the development and promotion of employees with disabilities. Cornelia: "My visually impaired colleague was told by her supervisor that the chance of a promotion are slim, because the processes at the higher level will not be accessible for her".

The fact that employees of particular departments of the company providing services to clients use various IT tools, which are only partially or sometimes not at all compatible with the screen reading programmes, used by visually impaired workers, was not taken into account. Cornelia: "I needed the support from other people practically for everything. System for submitting leave applications – not available, e-learning training – not available. Not to mention the fact that at some point the customer for whom we provided the service decided to change tools for work, and these new tools proved to be unavailable to me, which meant that I could no longer fulfil my current duties".

In addition, the extensive structure of the company and the complexity of corporate processes blocked the possibility of using reasonable improvements. Cornelia: "The project manager wanted to buy a plug-in for my software that would allow me to use work tools. The plug costs PLN 600, unfortunately its inclusion in the package of software provided to the project's employees was valued at $2000. And the topic was closed".

As a result, Cornelia gave up her job at the company, and good practices in the employment of people with disabilities, of which the organisation was proud, proved to be doubtful from the point of view of Cornelia.

Cornelia's case study was collected in 2019.

Cornelia's case shows two sides of good practices: positive and negative. It is important to analyse the effectiveness of good organisational practices taking into account the macro, meso and micro perspective (which we wrote about in Chapter 3). Sometimes what is good for the organisation is not always beneficial from the perspective of the individual employee. Hence, it is necessary to monitor and evaluate good practices. Sociological imagination, written about by the British sociologist Charles Wright Mills (1970), dealing with practical applications of sociology in social life is also very useful here.

Relevance and effectiveness of HRM solutions addressed to people with disabilities depend on the preparation of a coherent and comprehensive programme addressed to the employee as an individual. Fragmented of solutions, isolated processes and attempting to achieve goals impossible to achieve with a specific tool will result in low effectiveness of the organisation's activities and lack of employee satisfaction.

REFERENCES

Arczewska, Magdalena, Ewa Giermanowska, and Mariola Racław. 2014. "Pracodawcy i nowy model polityki społecznej wobec aktywności zawodowej osób niepełnosprawnych." In *Zatrudniając niepełnosprawnych. Dobre praktyki w Polsce i innych krajach Europy*, edited by Ewa Giermanowska, 96–114. Kraków: Akademia Górniczo-Hutnicza im. S. Staszica w Krakowie.

Brajer-Marczak, Renata. 2017. "Dobre praktyki w doskonaleniu procesów biznesowych." *Studia Informatica Pomerania* 1 (43): 15–24.

Bugajska, Joanna, Teresa Makowiec-Dąbrowska, and Ewa Wągrowska-Koski. 2010. "Zarządzanie wiekiem w przedsiębiorstwach jako element ochrony zdrowia starszych pracowników." *Medycyna Pracy* 61 (1): 55–63.

Code of Good Practice for the Employment of People with Disabilities, adopted by the Bureau of the European Parliament of 22 June 2005. Accessed February 25, 2019. http://www.europarl.europa.eu/pdf/disability/code_good_practice_en.pdf.

Giermanowska, Ewa, ed. 2014a. *Zatrudniając niepełnosprawnych. Dobre praktyki pracodawców w Polsce i innych krajach Europy*. Kraków: Akademia Górniczo-Hutnicza im. S. Staszica w Krakowie.

Giermanowska, Ewa. 2014b. "Zatrudnianie niepełnosprawnych pracowników. Oczekiwania pracodawców." In *Zatrudniając niepełnosprawnych. Dobre praktyki pracodawców w Polsce i innych krajach Europy*, edited by Ewa Giermanowskas, 61–95. Kraków: Akademia Górniczo-Hutnicza im. S. Staszica w Krakowie.

Giermanowska, Ewa. 2014c. "Dobre praktyki w zatrudnianiu osób niepełnosprawnych na polskim i europejskim rynku pracy." In *Zatrudniając niepełnosprawnych. Dobre praktyki pracodawców w Polsce i innych krajach Europy*, edited by Ewa Giermanowska, 15–40. Kraków: Akademia Górniczo-Hutnicza im. S. Staszica w Krakowie.

Grenier, Louis. 2017. "Death by 'Best Practices': Why They Can Kill Your Business." Last modified on 11 October 2017. Accessed February 2, 2019. https://www.hotjar.com/blog/death-by-best-practices?utm_source=Facebook&utm_campaign=BlogPromo_Facebook&utm_medium=display.

Hirschberg, Marianne, and Christian Papadopoulos. 2016. "'Reasonable Accommodation' and 'Accessibility': Human Rights Instruments Relating to Inclusion and Exclusion in the Labor Market." *Societies* 6 (3): 1–16.

Ilmarinen, Juhani. 2007. "The Work Ability Index (WAI)." *Occupational Medicine* 57: 160.

Ilmarinen, Juhani. 2009. "Work Ability—A Comprehensive Concept for Occupational Health Research and Prevention." *Scandinavian Journal of Work, Environment & Health* 35 (1): 1–5.

Kołodziej-Durnaś, Agnieszka. 2011. "Zarządzanie różnorodnością – inkluzja, innowacja czy instrumentalizacja?" In *Socjologiczne, pedagogiczne i psychologiczne problemy organizacji i zarządzania*, edited by Sławomir Banaszak and Kazimierz Doktór, 501–514. Poznań: Wydawnictwo Wyższej Szkoły Komunikacji i Zarządzania.

Kotzian, Joanna, Magdalena Pancewicz, and a team of consultants from HRK S.A. 2014a. "Rozdział I Praktyki polskie." In *Zatrudniając niepełnosprawnych. Dobre praktyki w Polsce i innych krajach Europy*, edited by Ewa Giermanowska, 117–216. Kraków: Akademia Górniczo-Hutnicza im. S. Staszica w Krakowie.

Kotzian, Joanna, Magdalena Pancewicz, and a team of consultants from HRK S.A. 2014b. "Rozdział II Praktyki zagraniczne." In *Zatrudniając niepełnosprawnych. Dobre praktyki w Polsce i innych krajach Europy*, edited by Ewa Giermanowska, 217–294. Kraków: Akademia Górniczo-Hutnicza im. S. Staszica w Krakowie.

Malińska, Marzena. 2017. "Ocena zdolności do pracy pracowników starszych wg WAI – wyniki wybranych polskich badań." *Bezpieczeństwo Pracy. Nauka i praktyka* 548 (5): 16–20.

Mills, Charles Wright. 1970. *The Sociological Imagination*. Harmondsworth: Penguin.

Paszkowicz, Maria. 2009. *Wybrane aspekty funkcjonowania osób z niepełnosprawnościami*. Zielona Góra: Uniwersytet Zielonogórski.

Pomagają niepełnosprawnym znaleźć pracę. Interview with Daria Uljanicka, board member of Integralna Foundation ERGO Hestia Foundation, by Anna Dobiegała 12 March 2018. Accessed April 1, 2019. http://trojmiasto.wyborcza.pl/trojmiasto/7,35612,23120753,pomagaja-niepelnosprawnym-znalezc-prace.html.

Report of the Municipal Public Library in Katowice for 2016. Accessed March 27, 2019. https://www.google.com/search?q=Sprawozdanie+Miejskiej+Biblioteki+Publicznej+w+Katowicach+za+rok+2016%2C+p.+1).&rlz =1C1GGRV_enPL751PL751&oq=Sprawozdanie+Miejskiej+Biblioteki+Publicznej+w+Katowicach+za+rok+2016%2C+p.+1).&aqs=chrome..69i57.1723j0j8&sourceid=chrome&ie=UTF-8.

Rutkowski, Krzysztof. 2006. "Zrozumieć fenomen najlepszych praktyk w logistyce i zarządzaniu łańcuchem dostaw. Europejskie wyzwania projektu BestLog." *Gospodarka Materiałowa i Logistyka* 12: 2–7.

von Schrader, Sarah, Valerie Malzer, and Susanne M. Bruyere. 2014. "Perspectives on Disability Disclosure: The Importance of Employer Practices and Workplace Climate." *Employee Responsibilities and Rights Journal* 26 (4): 237–255.

The Business Case for Diversity: Good Practices in the Workplace. 2005. European Commission Directorate-General for Employment, Social Affairs and Equal Opportunities Unit D.3. Luxembourg: Office for Official Publications of the European Communities.

Tran, Dung Anh. 2016. "Kiedy dobre praktyki są naprawdę dobre?" Blog audytorów śledczych EY. Last modified on 4 August 2016. Accessed February 2, 2019. https://www.blog.ey.pl/audytsledczy/kiedy-dobre-praktyki-w-biznesie-sa-naprawde-dobre/.

Ułamek, Ewa, Magdalena Pancewicz, and Joanna Kotzian. 2019. *Na zdrowie! Jak dbać o kondycję zdrowotną pracowników*. Warsaw: PWC.

Zakrzewska-Manterys, Elżbieta. 2008. "Piętno upośledzenia." In *O społeczeństwie, moralności i nauce. Miscellanea*, edited by Wojciech Pawlik, Elżbieta Zakrzewska-Manterys, 335–349. Warsaw: Uniwersytet Warszawski Instytutu Stosowanych Nauk Społecznych.

Ztroski o człowieka [Out of Concern for People]– Laboratorium Kosmetyczne Dr Irena Eris. No date. Accessed March 27, 2019. https://rodzinaipraca.gov.pl/dla-pracodawcy/dobre-praktyki/z-troski-o-czlowieka-laboratorium-kosmetyczne-dr-irena-eris/.

CHAPTER 6

Conclusions and Recommendations

Abstract Throughout this book, we explored the issue of the presence of people with disabilities in the open labour market. In the chapters, we analysed the multiple factors that contribute to the situation of disabled workers at work. We considered so-called good practices as one of the solutions in the hands of the employers that may aid the position of people with disabilities at work, to the benefit of employers, workers and the society at large. In this final chapter, we pull together the threads present throughout this book and present our final thoughts on the importance of the engagement of employers and workers in the creation of good jobs for a diverse population in the dynamically changing world of work and the creation and spread of good practices. We also consider the role and possible contribution of social scientists in the analysis, creation and implementation of good practices and appropriate policy, especially in relation to the larger political and social context.

Keywords Good practices in HRM ·
Factors influencing good practices among employers ·
Multivariate nature of good organisational practices ·
Scientific knowledge in changing the social world

People with disabilities constitute a large and heterogeneous population, facing the challenges of inclusion in the labour market. Experiences from many countries indicate the need to implement comprehensive and inclusive policies that relate to demand and supply on the labour market, addressed to employers as well as people with disabilities. Promoting the inclusion of disabled people on the labour market requires universal and, if necessary, specialized services, as well as promoting an environment that is more conducive to decent work for people with disabilities (ILO/OECD 2018).

Rapid social, demographic and technological changes affecting the labour market around the world create new challenges and opportunities for people with disabilities. The recently published World Bank (2019) and International Labour Office (2019) reports on changes in the nature of work and its future stress that work is constantly being transformed by technological progress. Artificial intelligence, automation and robotics create new jobs, but also there will be people who will have to adjust their qualifications, and this requires the support of public authorities. For people with disabilities, changes in the nature of work can be an opportunity, provided they are properly prepared for entering the labour market. The World Bank report draws attention to investing in human capital, which must be a priority for governments so that employees can build their skills on the labour market. It underlines the active role of governments in strengthening social protection and extending it to all people in society, regardless of the conditions in which they work (World Bank 2019). The ILO report calls for decisive action to improve the quality of professional life through among others reinvigorating the social contract: "Forging this new path requires committed action on the part of governments as well as employers' and workers' organizations" (ILO 2019, p. 10). It proposes an agenda that will strengthen the social contract by placing people and the work they perform at the centre of economic and social policy and business practice: This agenda consists of the following three pillars of action, which in combination would drive growth, equity and sustainability: (1) Increasing investment in people's capabilities, (2) Implementing a transformative and measurable agenda for gender equality and (3) Providing universal social protection from birth to old age (ILO 2019, pp. 11–13).

The role of investment in human capital and lifelong learning is growing in the new world of work. Hence, it is necessary to create and implement incentives addressed to disabled people and employers, develop institutional services sector supporting the entry and retention of disabled people in the labour market, as seek new, innovative forms of support. Good practices of employers implementing successful solutions in the employment of people with disabilities are one of the ways to increase employment in this social category, responding to the challenges of the modern labour market and the expectations of societies in economically developed countries.

At the same time, the analysis of good practices indicates the need to ask a more fundamental question about what "good work" is. Employers' measures directed to disabled employees, that are called good practices, show the illusiveness of the idea of defining a good job from the managerial perspective and in the economic efficiency category. "Good work", in the case of this social category, is associated above all with the satisfaction of employees, even those occupying subordinate positions in organisations and performing simple work. Employees have a sense of performing tasks they want to get involved in, and the organisation gives them a certain degree of freedom in performing their duties and a feeling that they can count on rational adjustments to shape their own work. Similar observations are made by Barry Schwartz (2015), when he reminds us that financial bonuses and strict supervision of managers over subordinates doing work in a routine manner are not enough to arouse the involvement of employees and give them job satisfaction. The task of modern developed societies is to create good workplaces, that is places, where people can do a good job. Only then will organisations gain satisfied customers and loyal employees who will find meaning in their activities for their organisation.

1 THE IMPORTANCE OF DIFFUSION OF GOOD PRACTICES AND THE SOCIOCULTURAL CONTEXT

The examples of good practices presented in the previous chapter related to the employment of disabled people have proved that companies and institutions in Poland and Europe implement effective solutions and achieve successes. They are the result of a complex combination of factors. At the macro-level, their implementation is conditioned by the state policy and applicable legislation, in the form of national and international law. At the level of the organisation, good practices are associated with building the organisational culture and image of the organisation based on the principles of equal opportunities and non-discrimination and respecting the idea of diversity. They are manifested by the implementation and observance of these values and standards in all the personnel procedures described in the previous chapter: recruitment and induction, adaptation of the workplace and assistants, employee retention and development and disability management in the workplace (Table 1).

Table 1 Examples of good practices in various areas of HRM

HRM area	Examples of procedures/tools
Recruitment and job induction	• Non-application of generally separate recruitment practices in relation to able-bodied and disabled people, application of the principle of distinguishing the competencies and not the employment parity. The only exception is recruitment of employees with intellectual disability, when a legal guardian or job coach may be present during interviews. Similarly, a sign language interpreter may be present during interviews with deaf people. • The use of specific recruitment channels, i.e. cooperation with non-governmental organisations helping disabled persons or associating disabled people, cooperation with public, private or non-governmental institutions preparing people with disabilities to work or intermediating in their employment. • Signalling in press advertisements that the company/institution is a friendly environment for disabled people. • Establishment of a special position or team for disability management policy, which elaborates the principles of external and internal recruitment. • The use of pre-selection in the case of cooperation with institutions or organisations that are the source of disabled candidates for work. • Preparation and adjustment of the scope of tasks in the organisation to the competencies and health opportunities of employees, often after consultation with a doctor and the disabled person. • The application of extended time of induction for people with disabilities, often under the care of a job coach. • Application of various information management procedures dealing with employee's disability when introducing him or her to a new team: – making information secret and disclosing it only at the request of a disabled person, especially in a situation of invisible/hidden disability; – organizing training for employees with disabilities before the disabled person is accepted for work; – informing co-workers of the employee about their health situation, if there was a risk that it could affect their work, contacts with the team or if the vigilance of the team in relation to the worker's health is needed.
Adapting the workplace and assistantship	• Purchase of the appropriate equipment needed for people with sensory disabilities, e.g. Braille displays, speech synthesizers, speaking devices and software adapted for people with disabilities. • Adaptation of space to the requirements of a disabled person, e.g. appropriate marking of rooms and creation of appropriately wide passes for wheelchairs. • Adaptation of the communication system in the company, e.g. bypassing paper communication in the presence of people with visual disabilities in the company or simplifying messages in the case of people with intellectual disabilities, offering sign language courses for hearing employees and employing a sign language interpreter.

(continued)

Table 1 (Continued)

HRM area	Examples of procedures/tools
	• Flexibility of the form of employment and working time, e.g. introduction of flexible working time and introduction of remote work at the employee's request.
	• Adjusting the location of employment in the event of a permanent workplace with the employer to the needs of workers with disabilities, e.g. in the case of companies with branches, employment of employees in the branches closest to their place of residence.
	• Provision of transport to the workplace.
	• Providing personal assistance services (and paying for it).
Keeping the employee in employment and employee development	• The development of rehabilitation services at the workplace, which allows the employee to return to work in the event of a disability being acquired during the employment period; cooperation in the field of rehabilitation with health-care facilities.
	• Implementation of the procedure of monitoring the health of employees in the event of prolonged periods of absence at work.
	• Retraining the employee, transferring the employee to other positions corresponding to his current state of health and fitness, adjusted according to the guidelines of the occupational medicine doctor.
	• Financing or subsidizing the costs of private health insurance for employees.
	• Offering health services to employees purchased from the organisation's partner.
	• Organizing training for employees in the workplace or outside the workplace, guaranteeing the necessary adjustments.
	• Co-financing of trainings by the employer and from other funds allocated for improving the qualifications of disabled employees.
	• Availability of information about training and vacancies at the workplace.
	• Encouraging disabled employees to raise their professional qualifications and standing.
	• Evaluating the performance of disabled employees according to the same criteria as those applied to employees performing the same or similar work.
	• Supervising the management process of a disabled employee by HR departments.
Disability management in the workplace	• Cooperation and communication with organisations representing employees and employees themselves, including people with disabilities, in order to present and approve disability management strategies.
	• Comprehensive and coherent actions in the field of internal policy related to the management of disability issues, with activities outside the organisation (e.g. CSR).

(continued)

Table 1 (Continued)

HRM area	Examples of procedures/tools
	• Increasing the level of awareness of all employees and managers in the field of disability issues, e.g. through trainings, workshops and internal communications addressed to employees of the organisation. • The use of knowledge of other specialized institutions dealing with disability issues or expert groups. • Disseminating information about good practices related to the employment of disabled people among other employers, their contractors and the local environment. • Research dealing with the effectiveness of policies for disabled people, publishing research results and correcting errors.
Employer's image and disability	• Using the fact of employing disabled people as part of the communication strategy at the global level (in the case of companies with many international branches) as well as at the local level (e.g. using appropriate formulas in recruitment advertisements); however, some companies avoid using the image of disabled employees due to the industry or sector in which they operate (e.g. insurance companies or high-ranking public organisations). • Participation in competitions designed for employers developing their personnel policies. • Participation in industry conferences and communication of their mission, conducting training for employers regarding the employment of disabled people. • Participation in conferences for people with disabilities. • Running or participating in meetings aimed at increasing the social awareness of the external environment, e.g. students of local universities. • Establishment of own non-governmental organisations that deal with activities supporting vocational activation of disabled people, financing scholarships for vocational education and training for people with disabilities, sponsoring activities corresponding to the company's profile of activities related to disability. • Building employees' social awareness through internal communication, e.g. placing information on employee rights on the intranet or conducting actions and training and regular employee satisfaction survey. • Creating and disseminating catalogues of good practices, brochures on CSR activities or referring to business ethics. • Transparency of employment information, including matters related to people with disabilities.

Source Own analysis

At the individual level, what is important for the occurrence of good practices is the attitude of the management and able-bodied and disabled employees and being open to change. Hence, the importance of knowledge delivery and promotion of successful solutions in the diffusion of good practices.

All initiatives, to be effective, must take into account the diversity of situations of disabled people, ensure equal treatment of women and men with disabilities and not exclude—if there are no rational indications—candidates for work due to their type and degree of disability. The condition for the success of personnel strategies including people with disabilities in the labour market is their comprehensive character, i.e. the concern for workers with disabilities should permeate all personnel processes. The use of selected tools to improve one personnel process, bypassing its relationship with others, leads to fragmented and isolated activities. They do not create holistic solutions that would respond to the dynamics of the employee's needs in his life cycle and in relation to changes in health. Activities for the disabled people employed, introduced incidentally and isolated from each other create dubious organisational practices, even if they can be used as a tool to improve the image of the employer or to make it look like a responsible business.

The implementation of good practices is associated with a broad sociocultural context. In Poland, in which the medical model is deeply rooted in defining the phenomenon of disability, such practices were perceived as something unique, atypical, poorly institutionalized in social perception. Studies in Western Europe have shown that they are much better rooted there and present in the personnel policy of companies and institutions. However, in Central and Eastern Europe as well as in Western Europe, there are difficulties in disseminating good organisational practices. They arise from multivariate conditions. Figure 1 approximates the complexity and multiplicity of influences that shape good organisational practices.

We refer here to our mode of multilevel and multi-variate conditions of employing people with disabilities presented in Chapter 3. We recognize the analogy of the complexity of the process of professional activation and employment of disabled people and the production of good practices in the employment of people with disabilities.

The nature of the phenomenon of disability (complexity, dynamics, intersectionality) determines the characteristics of disability management at the workplace. It can be supported by programmes for diversity, well-being and CSR functioning in the organisation.

Fig. 1 Factors influencing good practices among employers (*Source* Own analysis)

However, these cannot replace a well-thought-out employee management strategy because their goals are different from those set out in the perspective of disability. The ultimate goal of personnel policy in relation to people with disabilities is to introduce into the organisation and retain an employee with appropriate competences (understood as a triad: knowledge-attitude-skills). Good practices in this area should be treated as inspirational tips for innovations tailored to the specific company. Their self-regulatory nature promotes the creation of friendly work environments in a given labour market. However, we should not consider good practice as the only or sufficient mechanism for regulating employment processes on national or local labour markets. There is also a need for top-down regulators and activities facilitating the process of disabled people entering the open labour market. In our opinion, only the combination of effective and accurate public policy and bottom-up good practices will determine the integrative character of contemporary labour markets (Fig. 2).

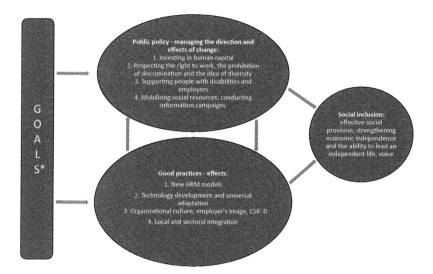

Fig. 2 Multivariate nature of good organisational practices. *(a) preparing people with disabilities for entering the labour market and retaining employment and (b) preparing employers to employ people with disabilities (*Source* Own analysis)

2 Scientific Knowledge and Its Importance in Changing the Social World

Finally, it is worth considering the role of science and scientists in interpreting the phenomenon of disability and changing the social world. Vic Finkelstein, when asked about the role of scientists in the development of interpretations of disability, pointed to the positive but limited impact of scientists and academic knowledge: "I don't think university academics can lead an emancipatory movement by promoting themselves as the sole developers of disability interpretations but I do feel they can have a positive influence and feed the hunger for knowledge that accompanies struggles against oppression. This requires a healthy link between academics, campaigners and disability organisations" (Finkelstein 2001, pp. 14–15). Solutions for people with disabilities and dealing with the phenomenon of disability must be developed with the participation of disabled people.

In this context, it is worth referring to the concept of sociology as a science in the perspective of Michael Burawoy and his postulate of the development of public sociology. The aim of researching good practices dealing with the employment of people with disabilities is to look for ways to increase the professional activity of people in this social category and to spread the belief (through the presentation of specific cases) that a multidimensional benefit can be derived from this: on an individual, organisational and social level. For a sociologist, this type of research, apart from cognitive and diagnostic value, is always of practical value, combined with applied and sometimes engaged sociology. Referring to the concept of Burawoy (2005), who lists four functions of sociology: theoretical, critical, practical and public and poses questions: Sociology for what? and Sociology for whom? This issue becomes an important challenge for social sciences.

The friction between the old (medical/individualistic model) and new (social and biopsychosocial model) assumptions about disability translates into the design of research procedures. Despite the objections to the social model (see Crow 1996), researchers increasingly reject the individualistic model and seek a new theoretical and methodological framework for explaining and understanding the phenomenon of disability (see Kowalska et al. 2014). They refer to the findings of critical sociology (see Hosking 2008) or public sociology (Burawoy 2005). As a result of this research, Disability Studies were established as a separate interdisciplinary and multidisciplinary reflection on disability as a sociocultural and political phenomenon, produced in everyday social practices. Disability Studies have been practised in the world for over three decades. "Disability Studies has its political and intellectual roots in the disability rights movement that began in the United States and the United Kingdom in the mid-twentieth-century and, by the turn of the twenty-first century, expanded to include other countries such as Canada and Australia, various countries in Europe and South America, and countries in South and East Asia" (Rembis and Pamuła 2016, p. 5). In Central and Eastern Europe, Disability Studies is a new area of research, and so far there have been few research and scientific centres, programmes and journals that would regularly address this issue or apply such a perspective (Pamuła et al. 2018, p. 7).

Breaking with the functionalist paradigm and drawing on the conflict theories of society, the supporters of Disability Studies postulate a new style of sociological profession. It is characterized by the recognition of the competences of the respondents, avoiding imposing the conceptual network of the researcher and abandoning the role of anonymous, neutral, academic experts (Kowalska et al. 2014, p. 232). The research methods and techniques used so far, referring to the individual/medical disability model, seem too paternalistic, hierarchical and exploitative in relation to the interlocutors. Objectivity and distance of a professional are being questioned as a manifestation of expert-researcher domination in the data collection process (Winogrodzka 2013). The new methodology is to facilitate not only obtaining information expressed on the basis of partnerships between respondents and researchers and participation of interviewees, it should also enable identification of their omissions and reconstruction of relations power and domination behind the social mechanisms of disability reproduction. The research is to lead to real changes in the lives of the respondents, because Disabilities Studies are embedded in the emancipatory and activist trend. It is not only an academic field, but also an influence tool (Zdrodowska 2016, p. 391). The ideal is to put the research process in the hands of disabled researchers and respondents, which is a testimony to its "emancipatory character" and a good move in terms of image creation. It also allows us to bring new sensitivity of non-disabled people to the research process, "so that the image of the phenomenon of disability is not created solely by able researchers, some of whom claim the right to define and describe what is not their experience" (Pamuła et al. 2018, p. 4). As a result, there should be a pressure of social change to make people with disabilities participate in principle in all social institutions, including the open labour market.

Sociological knowledge and a critical look at the solutions applied so far in the field of employment of disabled people in some countries, e.g. in Poland, often lead to many pessimistic statements regarding public policy: discrepancies between the declared principles and objectives and the actual way of implementing public activities (Gąciarz 2014), a closed system and an unused window of opportunity (Dudzińska 2015), an unfinished process of emancipation of disabled people as a result of blocking their access to the labour market (Giermanowska et al. 2015), the policy of expected failure (Kubicki 2017).

On the other hand, the involvement of sociologists and other scientists in activities for the benefit of the disabled through the diagnosis of the phenomenon, formulating conclusions and developing recommendations, as well as implementing and disseminating practical solutions (including good practices), create conditions for the emergence of social change. Of course, any research activity should be accompanied by critical reflection. Gathering knowledge about good/best practices in business or public activities is accompanied by the critical points mentioned in previous chapters related to their definition, purpose and criteria of choice, problems with their evaluation, transfer and communication. The practical use of good practices depends on the possibilities and conditions of their implementation. Successful organisations with good practice patterns, as Mary Jo Hatch (1997) emphasizes, sending signals about it to their environment, obtain, in this way, additional social legitimization necessary to attract resources to themselves. Through good practices, they can mobilize and control the activities of other companies that will imitate successful organisations (Hatch 1997). However, it should be taken into account that the context is important in the implementation of good practices, which means that unproven "best" solutions might not be successful in every context. When promoting and disseminating good practices, one should remember about their recipients, their needs and possibilities, as well as the conditions in which they are to be implemented. Scientific research also yields unobvious results regarding the effectiveness of good organisational practices. An example is the conclusions from research on inequalities in the workplace, the effectiveness of affirmative action methods and equality policy addressed to women and minority groups in American companies. The best results were achieved by assigning managers responsibility for organisational changes, while various types of training and feedbacks, as well as activities such as mentoring and networking aimed at reducing the social isolation of women and minority groups, brought much more modest results (Kalev et al. 2006). Conclusions from the research have emphasized that the influence of factors levelling inequalities in the workplace is closer to the classical sociology of the organisation than to the cognitive theories dealing with prejudices or social networks (Kalev et al. 2006, p. 611).

At the same time, it is worth emphasizing that research practice and organisational practice are guided by different logic of action and do not always lead to convergent results. The presented studies of good practice and our research experience lead to the conclusion that the effort put into their elaboration and dissemination is appreciated more in academic circles than among representatives of employers and public authorities. Employers generally remain passive, and only some of them are open to new initiatives related to the employment of disabled employees. For example, public policy in Poland regarding professional activation and employment of disabled people is conducted in line with the strategy developed in the 1990s which although ineffective, has a strongly institutionalized "strength of durability" (Giermanowska 2014, 2018; Gąciarz 2014; Barczyński and Habich 2018). The reasons for this are complex, and the lack of researchers' ability to communicate with employers and decision-makers does not facilitate this process. This phenomenon has been noticed in other countries. An example of this is the results of a literature analysis concerning the involvement of employers in specific employment practices for disabled people and their professional development, made in the United States after the implementation of the Act on Disabled Americans (concerning the period 1990–2011). The analysis proved that the majority of this literature was written for a group of people supporting disability and providers of rehabilitation services (state professional and social rehabilitation), instead of managers or personnel dealing with human resources or decision-makers. The articles were available mainly in rehabilitation and advocacy journals, and the focus was not on dissemination of knowledge among employers and HR departments (*Employer Practices and the Employment of People with Disabilities: Scoping the Literature* 2013). This phenomenon certainly applies to Poland and is a challenge for sociologists. How to communicate research and analysis results to employers and decision makers and to contribute more effectively to improving the living and working conditions of vulnerable groups?

The above observations also pose questions about the researchers' responsibility for the research process and the dissemination of its results. Undoubtedly, researchers should be attentive to the emerging restrictions during its duration. They do not work in a social vacuum. Particular challenges are created by the change of the scientific paradigm and, together with it, the transformation of political strategies, supported by new expert findings based on scientific evidence. That is the case of considerations about the nature of disability. Limitations related to the political dimension (alongside scientific, organisational and ethical limitations) to which social research projects are subject become important (Babbie 2001). Scientific reliability and diligence in preparing the research process, so that it is possible to carry it out according to certain assumptions and maintaining ethical standards, are not enough. It is necessary to be aware of the impact of policy on research as well as the results of research on policy. Research always takes place in a specific political context that generates research problems, but it can also distort the process of obtaining data or interpretations of the authors of research reports. Just as some people's problems are politicized, that is, they are perceived and perpetuated in terms of the interest of the authorities (Królikowska 2006), so also research activity may become politicized, even in democratic societies. Sometimes, it is the case that practising science or conducting research can lead the researcher into the middle of a violent political dispute, and researchers are automatically "drawn" into discussions about the assessment of the current political situation. At the same time, the intensity of the discussion on current events may obscure the original interpretations of results and prove to be countereffective in the creation of new solutions for the category of people being researched. This requires researchers to have a high degree of sociological imagination, attentiveness and a healthy scepticism of the offered schemas of interpretation of social events, presented suggestively by the community or their leaders, on whose behalf they carry out a deconstruction and social demystification. Solutions should help people and not organisations or interest groups in their survival, and with this in mind, we have been conducting an analysis of good practices of employing disabled people on the open labour market.

References

Babbie, Earl. 2001. *The Practice of Social Research*. Belmont, CA: Wadsworth/Thomas Learning.

Barczyński, A., and D. Habich. 2018. "Polityka wobec niepełnosprawności: pomiędzy rehabilitacją, aktywizacją zawodową i inkluzją społeczną." In *Stulecie polskiej polityki społecznej 1918–2018*, edited by E. Bojanowska, M. Grewiński, M. Rymsza, and G. Uścińska. Warszawa: MRPiPS, NCK.

Burawoy, Michael. 2005. "For Public Sociology." *American Sociological Review* 70: 4–28.

Crow, Liz. 1996. "Including All of Our Lives: Renewing the Social Model of Disability." In *Exploring the Divide: Illness and Disability*, edited by Colin Barnes, Geof Mercer, 55–73. Leeds: The Disability Press.

Dudzińska, Agnieszka. 2015. *System zamknięty: socjologiczna analiza procesu legislacyjnego*. Warszawa: Wydawnictwo Naukowe Scholar.

Employer Practices and the Employment of People with Disabilities: Scoping the Literature. 2013. Research presented at the Innovative Research on Employer Practices: Improving Employment for People with Disabilities, October, Washington.

Finkelstein, Vic. 2001. "A Personal Journey into Disability Politics." First presented at Leeds University Centre for Disability Studies, 1–15. Internet Publication. Accessed February 14, 2019. http://www.independentliving.org/docs3/finkelstein01a.pdf.
Gąciarz, Barbara. 2014. "Przemyśleć niepełnosprawność na nowo. Od instytucji państwa opiekuńczego do integracji i aktywizacji społecznej." *Studia Socjologiczne* 2 (213): 15–42.
Giermanowska, Ewa, ed. 2014. *Zatrudniając niepełnosprawnych. Dobre praktyki pracodawców w Polsce i innych krajach Europy.* Kraków: Akademia Górniczo-Hutnicza im. S. Staszica.
Giermanowska, Ewa. 2018. "Dobre praktyki w zatrudnianiu osób niepełnosprawnych w praktykach organizacji i doświadczeniu badawczym." *Societas Communitas* 26 (2): 63–83.
Giermanowska, Ewa, Kumaniecka-Wiśniewska Agnieszka, Racław Mariola, and Zakrzewska-Manterys Elżbieta. 2015. *Niedokończona emancypacja. Wejście niepełnosprawnych absolwentów szkół wyższych na rynek pracy.* Warszawa: Wydawnictwo Uniwersytetu Warszawskiego.
Hatch, Mary Jo. 1997. Organisational Theory: Modern, Symbolic and Postmodern Perspectives. Oxford: Oxford University Press.
Hosking, David L. 2008. "Critical Disability Theory." A paper presented at the 4th Biennial Disability Studies Conference at Lancaster University, UK, September 2–4. Dostęp August 21, 2018. http://www.lancaster.ac.uk/fass/events/disabilityconference_archive/2008/papers/hosking2008.pdf.
ILO/OECD. 2018. "Labour Market Inclusion of People with Disabilities." Paper presented at the 1st Meeting of the G20 Employment Working Group 20–22 February 2018, Buenos Aires, Argentina.
Kalev, A., F. Dobbin, and E. Kelly. 2006. "Best Practices or Best Guesses? Assessing the Efficacy of Corporate Affirmative Action and Diversity Policies." *American Sociological Review* 71: 589–617.
Kowalska, Beata, Agnieszka Król, Aleksandra Migalska, and Marta Warat. 2014. "Studia nad niepełnosprawnością a wyobraźnia socjologiczna." *Studia Socjologiczne* 2 (213): 225–250.
Królikowska, Jadwiga. 2006. "Przedmowa." In *Problemy społeczne w grze politycznej*, edited by Jadwiga Królikowska, 7–16. Warszawa: Wydawnictwo Uniwersytetu Warszawskiego.
Kubicki, Paweł. 2017. *Polityka publiczna wobec osób z niepełnosprawnościami.* Warszawa: Oficyna Wydawnicza SGH.
Pamuła, Natalia, Magdalena Szarota, and Marta Usiekniewicz. 2018. "Nic o nas bez nas." *Annales Universitatis Paedagogicae Cracoviensis. Studia de Cultura* 10 (1): 4–12.
Rembis, Michael, and Natalia Pamuła. 2016. "Disability Studies: A View from Humanities." *Człowiek -Niepełnosprawność - Społeczeństwo* 1 (31): 5–23.

Winogrodzka, Dominika. 2013. "Badacz/ka wobec doświadczenia. Studia nad niepełnosprawnością." Accessed August 15, 2018. http://krytyka.org/badaczka-wobec-doswiadczenia-studia-nad-niepelnosprawnoscia/#_ftn1.

Work for a Brighter Future—Global Commission on the Future of Work. 2019. Geneva: International Labour Office.

World Bank. 2019. *World Development Report 2019: The Changing Nature of Work*. Washington, DC: World Bank.

Schwartz, Barry. 2015. *Why We Work?* New York: Simon & Schuster/Ted.

Zdrodowska, Magdalena. 2016. "Między aktywizmem a akademią. Studia nad niepełnosprawnością." *Teksty Drugie* 5 (160): 384–403. Accessed August 20, 2018. Accessible on the Internet. http://rcin.org.pl/Content/62963/WA248_82836_P-I-2524_zdrodowska-miedzy_o.pdf. https://doi.org/10.18318/td.2016.5.25.

Index

A
Assistive Technologies (AT), 40, 41, 133

B
"Bundle of factors" model, 58

C
Convention on the Rights of Persons with Disabilities (CRPD), 12, 14, 111
Corporate Social Responsibility (CSR), 74–78, 82, 84, 86, 102–104, 110, 115, 119, 122, 125, 127, 128, 132, 133, 144, 145
CSR-D, 77, 78

D
Determinants, 11, 34, 37, 45, 53, 55, 56
 of the employment policy of disabled people, 6, 28
Disability management, 7, 26, 70, 71, 102, 116, 118, 121, 122, 141–143, 145

Disability studies, 10, 61, 148
Diversity management, 2–4, 7, 60, 69, 74, 76, 79–83, 122, 126, 131, 132
Documents of employment of disability people
 European Union (EU), 6, 11, 17
 International Labour Organization (ILO), 6, 18, 27, 70, 73, 88, 122
 United Nations (UN), 6, 11
 World Health Organization (WHO), 6, 18, 88

E
European models of employment of disability people
 quota system (redistributive, share), 24
 system based on civic rights (anti-discrimination, libertarian), 24
Exclusion from the labour market, 44
 non-employment of people with disabilities, 37

F

Factors
  from various levels of social organisation affecting the activity of people with disabilities, 58, 59
  influencing good practices among employers, 1
  research of activity of people with disabilities on the labour market, 28, 48

G

Good practices, 1–3, 5, 7, 8, 16, 25, 26, 30, 60, 67, 70, 72, 77, 82–92, 97–102, 106, 111, 116, 122, 126, 127, 130–132, 134, 139–142, 142–144, 148–150, 152
  adapting the workplace and assistantship, 8, 101, 111, 142
  definition, 83, 85
  disability management in the workplace, 7, 8, 97, 101, 122, 141
  employer's image and disability, 8, 101, 126, 144
  keeping the employee in employment and employee development, 8
  multivariate nature of good organisational practices, 145
  negative side of good practices, 8, 130, 134
  recruitment and induction, 8, 101, 102, 141, 142
  research of good practices, 7, 87, 88, 101
  at work, 3, 4, 87

H

Human resources management (HRM)
  functions, 67
  international documents, 6, 7, 70
  of people with disabilities, 131

I

International Classification of Functioning (ICF) conceptualization, 43, 44
International Classification of Impairments, Disabilities and Handicaps (ICIDH) conceptualization, 42–44

M

Model of disability
  biopsychosocial, 42
  medical, 39, 42, 149
  social model, 10, 11, 41, 42

R

Reasonable accommodation, 73, 111

S

Scientific knowledge in changing the social world, 147
Sociocultural context, 1, 8, 33, 141, 145
  and employment of disability people, 8, 141
  and good practices, 1, 141, 145
Statistics of employment of disability people, 23, 99

Printed by Printforce, the Netherlands